THINK HISTORY

CHANGING TIMES
1066–1500

Martin Collier Steve Day Barry Doherty Bill Marriott

Series editor: Lindsay von Elbing

FOUNDATION

heinemann.co.uk
✓ Free online support
✓ Useful weblinks
✓ 24 hour online ordering

01865 888080

Inspiring generations

Heinemann Educational Publishers
Halley Court, Jordan Hill, Oxford, OX2 8EJ
Part of Harcourt Education

Heinemann is the registered trademark of
Harcourt Education Limited

© Martin Collier, Steve Day, Barry Doherty, Bill Marriott, 2003.

First published 2003
07 06 05 04 03
10 9 8 7 6 5 4 3 2 1

British Library Cataloguing in Publication Data is available from the British Library on request.

ISBN 0 435 31330 4

Produced by IFA Design Ltd
Printed in Spain by Mateu Cromo s.a.
Picture research by Frances Topp
Illustrations on page 116 by Paul Bale

Photographic acknowledgements
The authors and publisher would like to thank the following for permission to reproduce photographs:
Aerofilms: 66A; AKG: 44C, 183C, 196C; Alamy: 79B; Ancient Art and Architecture: 20D, 29 (top), 103B, 104C; Ancient
Art and Architecture/L. Ellison: 8C; Art Archive: 78A, 142B; Art Archive/British Library: 157E; Bibliothèque Nationale
de France: 148E, 191F, 192G; Bridgeman: 79C, 85F, 107C, 174 (bottom) 196B; Bridgeman/House of Commons: 149F;
British Library: 113A, 137A, 137B, 141A, 148D; British Library/Bridgeman: 57A (Cott. Faust B VII f.72v); British
Museum: 146A; Cambridge University: 193I; Corbis: 10B, 17A; Corpus Christi College, Cambridge: 154C;
Courtauld/Conway Library/Corpus Christi College, Cambridge: 148C; Dean & Chapter of Durham Cathedral: 57B;
English Heritage: 48–9, 69A; Fortean Picture Library: 129A; Fotomas: 90B; Getty News: 153A; Hampshire Court
Records: 185F; Hulton: 156D, 178C, 191E, 192H; Lambeth Palace Library, London: 117C; Mansell Collection: 50A;
Mary Evans Picture Library: 38A; Michael Holford: 66C, 103A; NASA: 10A; PA News: 153B; Penshurst Palace: 164B;
Peter Evans: 163A; Photofusion: 93B, 93C; Rex: 24A; Robert Estall Photos: 66B; Robert Harding: 180F; Scala: 190C;
Sheridan/Ancient Art and Architecture: 83E; Sonia Halliday: 104D, 123B, 127F, 166E; Trinity College Cambridge: 98A;
Trip: 93A
Source unknown: 19B, 20C, 22E, 29 (bottom), 30, 40, 89A, 107A, 107B, 108D, 117B, 147B, 174A, 177A

Cover photograph: © British Library. The picture is 'An army being transported in ships', c. fifteenth century.

Written source acknowledgements
The author and publisher gratefully acknowledge the following publications from which written sources in the
book are drawn. In some sentences the wording or sentence structure has been simplified:
R. Allen Brown, *The Normans and the Norman Conquest* (Constable, 1968): 61D;
I. Coulson and I. Dawson, *Medicine and Health Through Time* (John Murray, 1996): 82D;
C. Culpin and I. Dawson, *The Norman Conquest* (John Murray, 2002): 70B;
J. Nichol, *Thinking History: Medieval Realms* (Blackwell, 1991): 82C;
S. Sancha, *Lincoln Castle: The Medieval Story* (Lincolnshire County Council, 1985): 71D;
ed. Lesley Smith, *The Making of Britain: The Middle Ages* (Macmillan, 1985): 165D, 167G;
A. Williams, *The English and the Norman Conquest* (Boydell, 1995): 60C

Tel: 01865 888058 www.heinemann.co.uk

CONTENTS

1 Did Harold deserve to lose the English throne?   5

2 Did William's conquest change England?   47

3 Was medieval medicine all 'doom and gloom'?   75

4 What were people's beliefs in the Middle Ages?   101

5 Who was the best and who was the worst king, 1087–1307?   133

6 What was life like in the Middle Ages?   161

DID HAROLD DESERVE TO LOSE THE ENGLISH THRONE?

You are about to go on a journey of discovery. By the end of this chapter, you will know and understand a lot more about a big crisis that affected England nearly 1000 years ago. You will be able to answer some key questions about this time.

💡 *Why have people always wanted to invade Britain?*

💡 *Why did the death of a king push England into war and chaos?*

TIMELINE
6500 BC to AD 1066

6500 BC	The first humans settle in the British Isles.
500 BC	The Celts begin to arrive from northern Europe.
AD 42	The Romans begin their invasion of Britain.
AD 360	Barbarian armies begin to invade Roman Britain.
AD 410	Roman Britain ends.
AD 750	The Vikings begin raids and set up control over northern and eastern England.
AD 937	King Athelstan restores Anglo-Saxon rule.
AD 980	The Danish Vikings attack England.
AD 1016	The first of three Viking kings begins to rule England.
AD 1042	King Edward the Confessor is the first English king in 26 years.
AD 1066	Harold Godwin is defeated at the Battle of Hastings by Duke William of Normandy.

WHO INVADED BRITAIN BEFORE 1066 AND WHY?

Objectives

By the end of this section you will be able to answer these questions.
- Why did early invaders want to invade Britain?
- Who invaded Britain between 500 BC and AD 1016?
- How did these invaders change Britain?
- How settled were the people of Britain before 1066?

Starter

With a partner, make a list of any nations you think have ever invaded Britain.

Britain: a land worthy of invasion?

Britain has not been invaded now for nearly 950 years. Many people do not realise that these lands were once an attractive destination for many invaders. The first human beings arrived in Britain about 8500 years ago. These Stone Age people were probably attracted by the large empty forests, filled with wild animals. They had also heard they could find precious metals like gold and silver.

SOURCE (A)

Most of the tribes do not grow grain. They live on milk and meat, and they wear animal skins. They dye their bodies with **woad**, which makes them look wild – especially in battle. They wear their hair long, but they shave every other part of their body, except the upper lip.

A description of the Celts in 55 BC by the Roman emperor, Julius Caesar.

Key words

Woad A plant that gives a blue dye.

The first large group of settlers were the Celts. They began to arrive around 500 BC. The Celts were well known for their unusual religious practices and their frightening appearance in battle.

Medieval Europe in 1066.

The next large group of settlers to arrive were the Romans. Between AD 42 and AD 84 they conquered England and Wales. They got as far as Hadrian's Wall, which was the border with Scotland.

Roman Britain was a peaceful and wealthy place for almost 300 years. The Romans built fine buildings, country houses, libraries and roads. But by the start of the fifth century, they were losing power. They left Britain, and other people began to invade.

The new invaders
The Anglo-Saxons

New invaders began to raid and then settle along the English coastline. Many came from Denmark and northern Germany. They were known as the Anglo-Saxons.

Key words

Scandinavia A group of countries that includes Denmark and Norway.

Viking Invaders from Scandinavia.

The Vikings

Invaders also came from **Scandinavia**. They were known as the **Vikings**. The Vikings were very good sailors and fierce warriors. They enjoyed sea voyages, war and making money from trading. Vikings from Norway began attacking England from about AD 750. Eventually they decided to settle in England and set up farms.

Throughout the tenth century, the old Anglo-Saxon armies slowly started to control Britain again. One of its leaders, Athelstan, was known as 'The King of All Britain'. He became the first person since the Roman emperors to rule the whole country.

Then more Danish Vikings began raiding the English. They conquered England for a second time. Between 1016 and 1042 three Viking kings, Canute and his two sons Harefoot and Harthacanute, ruled England.

In 1042 England was ruled by another Englishman, Edward the Confessor. But would he be the last English king? Or would England be attacked by another foreign army?

SOURCE C

Viking long ships, like this one, let the Vikings travel as far as Greenland and North America.

TASKS...

1 Look at these settlers who arrived in Britain between 6500 BC and AD 980. Put them in order to show which group arrived first. Write down your answer in your book.

Vikings   **Romans**   **Stone Age**   **Anglo-Saxons**   **Celts**

2 In pairs, make a list of questions you would like to ask to find out more about the early settlers in Britain. Compare your list with others.

Plenary

Work in pairs to complete the definitions table. The first person can pick any of the definitions. The second person should give the correct term for that definition. Now swap jobs!

DEFINITIONS	TERMS
Precious metals found in Britain.	Celts
It covered most of Britain one thousand years ago.	Christianity
A time when no one used metal.	Vikings
The first major group of settlers.	gold and silver
Built to keep the Scots out of England.	Hadrian's Wall
The last Viking king in Britain.	Stone age
A new religion brought by the Romans.	Anglo-Saxons
They came from Denmark and Germany.	Harthacanute
They enjoyed fighting and trading.	forest

You could also try choosing a term and working out the definition that goes with it.

WHAT WERE THE KEY EVENTS IN THE LIFE OF KING EDWARD?

Objectives

By the end of this section you will be able to answer these questions.
- Who was Edward the Confessor?
- How did he become king against all the odds?
- Did it matter that he had no children?
- Who became king when he died?
- Why was the new king such a problem?

SOURCE (A)

The first moon landing, 1969.

Starter

Look at Sources A and B below. They are both well-known moments in history.

SOURCE (B)

The terrorist attack on the World Trade Centre in New York, 11 September 2001.

💡 *Do you think these two events are important moments in history?*

💡 *How do you think people reacted to these two events?*

💡 *How do you think the world changed after these events?*

💡 *Do you think the world can change forever after a single event?*

How was Edward's life turned ndsɪpə poʌʌu?

The year 1066 is one of the most important in the history of Britain. Historians have described it as a *'watershed'* or *'turning point'* in history.

💡 What do you think these two words mean?

Read this story together as a class. Think about the questions at the end of each section. **WS**

Edward's early years

Prince Edward had a lot of royal blood. He was the son of Athlestan, King of all England. His mother, Emma, was the sister of a Norman duke. He had an older brother, Alfred, and a younger sister, Goda. Edward enjoyed a carefree childhood. But his happiness didn't last.

In 1013 and 1016, the **Danes** attacked England. The stress was too much for Edward's parents. His father died suddenly and his mother ran off to her brother in Normandy. She took her children with her. It was here that Edward spent the rest of his childhood, in a cold and draughty Norman castle.

💡 Why do you think Edward might have felt frightened in the Norman castle?

Edward's return to England

England was now ruled by a new king. He was a tough and fearless Viking called Canute. He had a son called Harefoot.

Emma's brother said she had to go back to England and marry Canute. She did this, and they had a son called Harthacanute.

In 1035 King Canute died. Canute's two sons began arguing about who would be the next king.

In the middle of all this arguing, Emma encouraged Alfred and Edward to return to England. She thought they should then claim the throne for themselves! Edward got as far as Southampton, but retreated. Alfred was not so lucky. He was captured by Earl Godwin's men and handed over to Harefoot. Alfred was then horribly murdered with a red-hot poker. Edward blamed **Earl** Godwin for his brother's death.

💡 Why do you think Edward and Alfred wanted to return to England?

Harefoot ruled England for five years, from 1035 to 1040. When he died Harthacanute ruled for two years, until 1042. They were the last Viking kings of England.

Edward marries

Edward was now free to claim the throne of England. When he arrived in England he quickly married Edith Godwin. She was the daughter of the most powerful and richest earl in England, who Edward blamed for his brother's death.

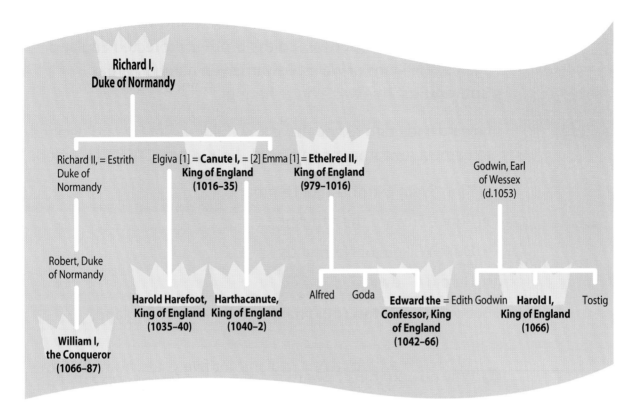

Family tree showing the links between the Norman and English families.

💡 Why do you think Edward married the daughter of his old enemy?

Edward and religion

In 1051, Edward fell out with the Godwin family. The Godwins were forced into hiding and poor Edith was imprisoned in a **convent**. But a year later Edward was forced to **pardon** the family. When Earl Godwin died the following year, Edward gave him a full state funeral, like that of a king.

💡 Why do you think Edward was forced to pardon the Godwin family?

The old hatred Edward felt towards the Godwins seemed to disappear. Harold Godwin, Edith's brother, protected England against the kings of Wales. Edward even named Harold **'subregulus'**. This was a huge honour.

Edward and Edith did not have any children. But Edward decided to name a few other people as his **heir** instead. These included:

- King Svein Estrithson of Denmark
- Prince Edward the Atheling
- Duke William of Normandy
- Harold Godwin.

But only the **Witan** could name a new king of England.

Why do you think Edward promised the throne to so many people?

Edward dies

On Christmas Eve 1065, Edward had a stroke. Harold, Edith and the Witan gathered around the king to hear his final words. Moments before he died, Edward looked at Harold and said,

'I give you this kingdom for you to protect'.

Harold had been named by Edward as his successor – the person to next take the throne of England. This choice was immediately backed by the Witan.

On 6 January 1066, Edward was buried and Harold was crowned King of England. But Harold's happiness was partly spoiled because he knew that many foreign kings and dukes were unhappy about his **coronation**.

Key words

Subregulus Deputy king.
Heir The person who will be the next king or queen.
Witan A council of noblemen that advised the king.
Coronation When a person is crowned king or queen.

TASKS...

1 You heard about a lot of people in Edward's story. Who is who? Write a sentence to explain what you now know about these people.

Edward	**King Ethelred**	**Earl Godwin**
Harefoot	**William**	**Edward the Atheling**

2 Below are some key moments in Edward's life. Use his story from pages 11-14 to arrange these events into chronological (time) order.

   (a) Edward hears of his brother's capture and horrific death.

   (b) Edward is forced to retreat from Southampton.

   (c) Edward's mother marries King Canute and has a son called Harthacanute.

   (d) Just before he dies, Edward names Harold Godwin as his successor.

   (e) Edward finally becomes king in 1042.

   (f) Edward and Edith do not have any children.

   (g) Edward's father dies and the family is forced to flee to Normandy.

   (h) Edward marries Edith Godwin in 1045.

   (i) The young Edward lives in London with his brother, sister, mother and father – who is King of England.

   (j) Edward grows up among strangers in a Norman castle.

3 Use statements (a) to (j) to make a living graph of Edward's life. Try to work out the happiest and saddest moments in his life.

Happiest moments ↑

Saddest moments ↓

Birth — Death

4 Find examples in the story of Edward's life that would suggest he was:

   • indecisive   • lonely   • lucky.

   • cruel   • frightened

   Put these headings in your book and summarise under each one, an example from the story of Edward's life.

Plenary

Unexpected things can happen to us that might change our lives forever. In pairs, write down at least two of these kinds of moments in Edward's life.

Compare your ideas with others in the class to create one big list. Use your big list to write down these moments in order of importance.

KEY CONTENDERS: WHO HAD THE GREATEST CLAIM TO THE ENGLISH THRONE?

Objectives

By the end of this section you will be able to answer these questions.

- How many **contenders** were there to the English throne?
- Why did each of them think he should be king?
- Whose claim to the throne was the greatest?

You will carry out a SWOT analysis to discover whose claim to the throne was the greatest.

Starter

In 1912, the Titanic *sank. On board were priceless pieces of jewellery, works of art, precious metals and other belongings worth millions of pounds. There were also the bodies of more than 1500 people who drowned.*

Key words

Contender Someone who is in competition with others for something.

SOURCE (A)

The *Titanic* sank in the Atlantic Ocean in 1912.

In pairs, look at Source A. Imagine that a very rich person has built a ship that can pull the Titanic *from the sea bed.*

💡 *List all the people who should be given a share of this fortune.*

💡 *Now choose the top three contenders for this fortune.*

On your own, decide who has the 'greatest claim' and who has the 'weakest claim' to this fortune. Jot down your reasons.

The main contenders to the throne

Just before he died in January 1066, King Edward the Confessor named Harold Godwin as his successor. The Witan backed Edward's choice. But at least three other men, William of Normandy, Prince Edgar the Atheling and Harald Hardrada, thought that Harold had no right to become king. They each thought they should be king! Now there were four contenders.

TASKS...

1 Choose which contender you think was the rightful King of England. Carry out a SWOT analysis on each one when you have read the information about that person. For each contender, copy out a chart like the one below. Give yourself plenty of room for the answers. **WS**

Name of contender:	
Strengths	*This is where you write out the claims of the contender.*
Weaknesses	*This is where you say why these claims might not be very strong.*
Opportunities	*This is where you write out any chances he has to become king.*
Threats	*This is where you write out any dangers faced by the contender.*

William of Normandy

William was a strong fighter. He never lost a single battle or failed to capture a castle before 1066. He claimed the throne of England for several reasons.

SOURCE B

William the Conqueror.

1 He was related to the kings of England. His great aunt (Emma) had been married to both King Ethelred and King Canute. So he was related to two previous kings of England – Edward the Confessor and Harthacanute.

2 He said that in 1051 Edward had named him as his successor.

3 He claimed that in 1064 Harold **swore an oath** to support William's claim to the throne when Edward died. In those days, people believed that you would burn in hell forever if you broke an oath!

The Normans had the best **cavalry** in Europe. Their horses were tall and fast. Their soldiers trained hard and were skilled in archery. William had the use of 30,000 trained soldiers. But the Normans did have one major weakness – their navy. They didn't have much knowledge or skills in this area.

Key words

Swear an oath To make a promise to God.

Cavalry The part of an army that fights on horseback.

Edgar Atheling.

Prince Edgar the Atheling

Prince Edgar was King Edward's closest relative. He was five years old when his father died and fourteen when his great uncle, King Edward the Confessor, died.

In 1057, King Edward named Edgar's father, Edward the Atheling, as his successor (see page 14). But on a visit to meet King Edward, Edward the Atheling died mysteriously.

Because Prince Edgar was very young, not many people thought he would be the next king. He had no money, no soldiers and no experience of battle. King Edward and the Witan did not think Prince Edgar was a good choice.

Key words

Civil war A war between two groups in one country.

Harald Hardrada.

Harald Hardrada

Harald was the son of a nobleman who ruled a small part of Norway. In 1030 he had to run away from Norway after the death of his uncle, King Olaf of Norway, in a fierce **civil war**.

Between 1034 and 1043, Harald led the Varangian Guard – a ruthless and feared army based in Turkey. For nine years, he cleared seas of pirates and fought battles in places like Israel, Africa and Sicily. By 1043, he was one of the most famous and experienced warriors in the world.

But Harald wanted to be king of Norway as well. In 1047, Magnus of Norway died and Harald did become king!

Some people believed that Vikings like Harald were the true kings of England. Harald liked the idea, but he never thought about England. All of that changed with the mysterious arrival of Tostig Godwin, Harold Godwin's brother, to Harald's court in Norway.

Tostig and Harold Godwin had quarrelled, and Tostig ran away from England to escape certain death. Tostig convinced Harald Hardrada that the people of northern England hated Harold Godwin and wanted the Vikings to return.

Harald had about 18,000 soldiers ready to fight and around 300 ships for the long crossing from Norway. Like the English, the Vikings preferred hand-to-hand combat rather than a cavalry. However, both **infantry** and horses could be taken if they were needed.

Harald also knew that his soldiers would have to rely on the kindness of the English for food. If they were not given food, they would have to steal it.

Key words

Infantry The part of an army that fights on foot.

Harold Godwin.

Harold Godwin

Harold's family had become very rich and powerful during the reign of King Canute. Harold's father had been made an earl in 1018. By 1066, the family had become the richest and most powerful in England.

From the late 1050s, King Edward relied on Harold to defend his kingdom. The biggest threat came from the kings of Wales. Harold finally crushed the Welsh armies in 1063.

Harold's only blood link to King Edward was his sister, Edith, who was married to the king. But in the eleventh century, blood relatives of a king did not automatically become the next king. Anyone could be king if they were chosen by the Witan.

Harold had been named by King Edward as subregulus, meaning 'deputy king'. Also, as Edward lay dying, he named Harold as king. In the Anglo-Saxon world the dying wishes of a king were considered **sacred**.

Harold's Anglo-Saxon warriors were skilled in hand-to-hand combat. They were good sailors, and a large navy patrolled the waters around the English Channel and the North Sea. Harold could have called on an army of 10,000 trained soldiers and 240,000 untrained peasants to fight.

Key words

Sacred Unbreakable, and even holy.

TASKS...

1 Using the results of your SWOT analysis, which person do you think had the strongest claim to the throne?

2 (a) Now look at the four things below. Give each contender a mark out of 10 for how well they score on each thing. 0 points is very bad, 10 points is very good. Copy out the chart and write in your marks. **WS**

	William	Edgar	Harald Hardrada	Harold Godwin
1 Experience of warfare				
2 Well trained army				
3 Good tactics				
4 Right to the English throne				
Totals				

   (b) Which of the four things listed do you think should be the most important? Discuss your answer with a partner.

3 Compare the results of your SWOT analysis with the scores in the chart. Have you changed your mind about who had the strongest claim to the throne? Take a class vote to see if the whole class agrees on the same person.

Plenary

The SWOT analysis is a good way of analysing situations.

Which other situations could you use a SWOT analysis for?

Perform a SWOT analysis on a situation from your own life. For example, you could use a SWOT analysis to decide where to go on holiday or for choosing a new home or car.

THE ALLEGED OATHS: DID HE OR DIDN'T HE?

Objectives

By the end of this section you will be able to answer these questions.
- Did Harold really swear an oath to support William?
- Why can't we be sure about what really happened in 1064?
- Why was Harold's oath so important to the Normans?

You will also look at what makes a reliable source and what makes a misleading one.

Starter

Look at Source A.

A witness in the stand in a modern-day court of law. Notice how her right hand is holding a copy of the Bible. She is about to take an oath: 'I swear to tell the truth, the whole truth, and nothing but the truth, so help me God'.

💡 *What is an 'oath'?*

💡 *Why do you think witnesses swear an oath before they are questioned by the court?*

💡 *Why do you think many people are afraid of telling lies after they have sworn an oath to God?*

The sacred oath

In the eleventh century almost everybody believed in God. They believed in heaven and hell.

People thought that one way to go to hell was to break a sacred oath. This means making a promise to God, then breaking that promise. People in those days believed that if you did this, your honour and your soul would be destroyed forever.

William claimed that both King Edward the Confessor and Harold Godwin had promised to support his claim to the throne. The **Pope** believed William and supported his claim. But were these promises really made? Did William deserve the throne of England?

Look at the storyboard here and on the next page to examine *the Norman version of events*. **WS**

Edward loved the Normans. His mother was Norman and the Normans had protected him as a child. In Normandy, he grew to admire William. They became great friends.

In 1051, King Edward thought about a successor. Edward's love of Normandy made him choose William as his heir. Edward offered him the crown of England when he died. Edward and all the earls of England swore an oath of loyalty to William. William came home and waited for the king to die. In 1064, Edward sent Harold Godwin to Normandy. He wanted to tell William that he hadn't changed his mind.

As Harold sailed to Normandy, a violent storm shipwrecked his fleet. Everyone apart from Harold drowned. A lighthouse keeper saved Harold. He took him to William.

Harold passed on Edward's message. He also swore a sacred oath to support William. Harold spent several months fighting and hunting with William. They became great friends.

💡 Which aspects of the story appear likely? Which appear unlikely?

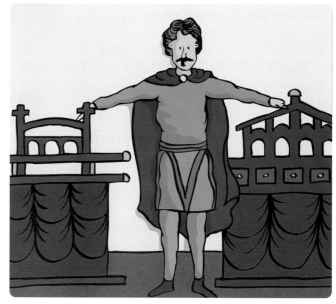

Did Harold really make the oath?

Key words

Alleged Something that someone is said to have done, but that hasn't been proven.

Most records of what happened were written after 1066. We can't be sure where people got their information about the **alleged** oath. So we can't be certain if Harold made an oath at all! Also, even if Harold did swear an oath, we can't be sure exactly what he promised to do.

TASKS...

In groups, answer questions 1 to 4 below. The answers to these questions will help you with writing an extended answer to question 5.

1 What did people think would happen if they broke a sacred oath?

2 What evidence is there that Harold *did* swear an oath in Normandy?

3 What evidence is there that Harold *did not* swear an oath in Normandy?

4 Find reasons why we can't trust the Norman version of events.

5 Use what you have found out from Tasks 1 and 2 to write an extended answer to the question:
'Did Harold Godwin swear an oath in support of William in 1064?'

Here is some advice to help you to write a good answer.

Introduction
You should write about the argument you are going to make in your answer. Explain why the oath was so important to the Normans.

First paragraph
Write about the evidence that suggests Harold did make an oath in 1064.

Second paragraph
Write about why we should be suspicious of the Norman evidence.

Conclusion
Decide if you should accept the Norman claims about this oath. You could also include some of the reasons why an oath might not have counted anyway.

> 💡 **TIP!**
>
> Each paragraph should have an attention-grabbing topic sentence!

Key words

Reliable Something that can be counted on or trusted.

Plenary
Read this chapter again to remind yourselves about sacred oaths? Do you think the evidence for a sacred oath is **reliable**? Give reasons for your answer. You will need to think about:

- what the evidence is
- who produced it
- why they produced it.

HOW DID EACH LEADER PREPARE FOR WAR?

Objectives

By the end of this section you will be able to answer these questions.

- What might Harold, William and Harald have been thinking in early 1066?

- Why did all three contenders to the throne believe they could win?

- Which contender had the strongest army?

Starter

Decisions, decisions ...

Imagine you are about to go on a long voyage of discovery to the Arctic Circle. Your adventure will last four weeks. You can only take five items from the list below.

tent	sleeping bag	gun/bullets	water	chocolate
dried food	gas stove	skis	sun cream	gloves/hat
binoculars	camera	mobile phone	sunglasses	first aid kit

Which items should you choose? On your own choose:

- *five items you really need*
- *five items you would use and would like*
- *five items you don't need but would like.*

Now share your decisions with other members of your class. Are your decisions the same? If they are different, why are they different?

Who would become king?

Remember the four contenders to the English throne?

They were:
- Prince Edgar
- William of Normandy
- Harald Hardrada
- Harold Godwin.

Only three of them had enough experience and power to try to become king. Edgar, the fourteen year-old prince, decided not to try. The remaining three contenders must have thought long and hard about the 'fors' and 'againsts' of becoming king. Look at pages 29 and 30 to see what might have been worrying them.

Housecarl A soldier, usually from Scandinavia, who was trained to protect Viking kings.

Omen A sign that something good or bad is about to happen.

💡 For all 3 contenders, which thoughts are *for* challenging the throne, and which are *against* challenging the throne?

What Harald Hardrada might have thought …

Some people hate Harold Godwin and would welcome another Viking king.

English **housecarls** are very frightening.

It's a dangerous journey to England.

When I win, I will be known as one of the greatest warriors in the history of the world.

I will become the richest man in the world.

I can't be sure the people of northern England will welcome me.

Godwin will have to fight William in the south, so I can take northern England without a fight.

What if Godwin beats William, then turns his whole army against us?

What William of Normandy might have thought …

We might run out of supplies when we get to England.

Norman cavalry, archers and infantry are very skilled.

Good **omens** prove God will make sure of our victory.

The English people see me as a foreigner. They will never accept me as their new king.

I might not get safely across the English Channel.

I have never lost a battle!

Godwin's forces are spread too thinly across England.

Godwin is a great warrior. He might beat me.

What Harold Godwin might have thought …

Harald and William will struggle to bring enough men to England.

I might have to fight two invaders at the same time.

If we are not attacked before September, I will have to send men home to collect in the harvests.

I can't trust some earls to support me.

The Normans can only bring supplies for a few weeks.

My navy might destroy the Norman army before it even sets foot on English soil.

Although I have a much bigger army, William's army is better trained.

The southern English people will fight to the death for me.

TASKS...

1 **(a)** Get into groups of three. Decide who will pretend to be Harold Godwin, William or Harald Hardrada.

   (b) Read through your person's thoughts again and remind yourself of their **dilemma**. It might help to remind you of their claim to the throne (see pages 18-22).

2 Now interview each other by putting 'Harald', 'William' and then 'Harold' in the hot seat. It might help to ask some of these questions.

   • Why do you think you should be king?

   • What makes you think you can win?

   • What doubts or worries do you have?

Key words

Dilemma A difficult choice or decision.

Who had the strongest army?

A member of the English fyrd.

Five facts about the English army

1 The army was divided into a small group known as the housecarls and a much larger group known as the fyrd.

2 The housecarls were fully trained **professional** soldiers.

3 The fyrd were less experienced and less well equipped.

4 The fyrd's usual job was farming.

5 The English preferred fighting with battle-axes.

An English housecarl.

Five facts about the Norman army

1 All the soldiers were fully trained professionals.

2 William also used **mercenaries**.

3 Soldiers carried two weapons – a sword and a spear.

A Norman infantry man.

4 William had hundreds of deadly archers and slingshots.

5 The army was supported by 5000 blacksmiths, carpenters, doctors and cooks.

A Norman cavalryman.

DID HAROLD DESERVE TO LOSE THE ENGLISH THRONE?

A Norwegian Viking.

Five facts about the Viking army

1 Between 12,000 and 18,000 men left Norway with Harald Hardrada.

2 Most of the soldiers were trained. Some were very experienced.

3 They liked surprise attacks launched from the coastline.

4 They preferred hand-to-hand fighting using axes and hammers.

5 They did not like to use horses in battle.

TASKS...

1 In pairs, choose either the English (Harold's men), Normans (William's men) or Vikings (Harald's men) to investigate. Read the text on pages 31–2. Then copy out the chart below. Give scores out of 10 for each category in the chart.

Army under investigation:

	Score out of 10	Advantages	Disadvantages
Armour			
Weapons			
Cavalry			
Archers and bowmen			
Training			

Write about the advantages and disadvantages for each category. Remember to give yourself enough space to write. Also remember to jot down on your chart whose army you are investigating. **WS**

2 (a) Look at the words in the grid below. Some of them might be used to describe Harald Hardrada, William or Harold Godwin.

daring	adventurous	unlucky	wealthy	cunning
deceptive	wise	organised	rash	foolish
trusting	ill-prepared	confident	unwise	lucky

TASKS...

(b) Choose two words from the grid to describe Harold Godwin's preparations for battle. Give reasons for your choice. Now do this for Harald Hardrada and William of Normandy.

(c) Discuss your choices with your neighbour or the class.

Plenary

Think about the armies of Harald, William and Harold.

- Which army would prefer a surprise attack?

- Which army would prefer to know about a battle?

- Which army would prefer to fight over a few days?

Be ready to give reasons for your answers.

HOW DID THE FIGHTING START AT FULFORD GATE, STAMFORD BRIDGE AND HASTINGS?

Objectives

By the end of this section you will be able to answer these questions.
- Who came out on top by the end of 1066 - Harald Hardrada, Harold Godwin or William the Conqueror?
- Was luck the most important thing in the battles of 1066?
- Did Harold deserve to be defeated at the Battle of Hastings?

Starter

ENGLAND 6 : BRAZIL 0

Imagine this is the final score of the next Football World Cup final. If you were to investigate the causes of this victory, you might be able to split them into three categories.

Make a chart in your book like the one below. Now read these statements. Put them into the correct place in your chart.

(a) Brazil's star player broke his leg in the semi-final.

(b) The Brazilian manager risked his seventeen year-old second-choice goalkeeper.

(c) The England manager decided on a traditional 4-4-2 formation.

(d) The Brazilian captain kept asking his players to go forward and defend less.

(e) All of England's best players were 100 per cent fit.

(f) The England players had practised winning the ball and counter-attacking.

This activity will help you later on when we analyse the events of the Battle of Hastings and try to answer the big question, 'Did Harold deserve to lose the Battle of Hastings?'

Good luck	Good decisions by England	Bad decisions by Brazil
This is when victory occurs because one side seems to have everything going in its favour.	This is when victory occurs because of good decisions or planning.	This is when victory occurs because the opponent makes errors or mistakes.
Examples	Examples	Examples
1.	1.	1.
2.	2.	2.

Preparations for war

Wars and battles are like games of football. The winning side has usually been lucky and made lots of good decisions. It also helps when the opposition has made bad decisions! As you read the information about the battles in 1066, make notes in answer to the short questions. Your notes need not be full sentences. Try to use key words, names and dates.

Getting ready

Harold Godwin expected an attack from spring 1066. Spies had told Harold that Harald Hardrada and William of Normandy were getting ships ready for their invasions.

By late August everything was still quiet. Harold Godwin felt the English could relax, so he let his fyrd army return home to collect the harvest.

But William was ready to attack. He had planned to attack in late July. But his boats were not very strong. So he had to wait until the sea was calm.

Fortunately for William, disaster struck the English. A storm destroyed most of the English navy.

- 💡 How did bad luck weaken the English?
- 💡 Do you think William's delayed departure was a good decision or just good luck?

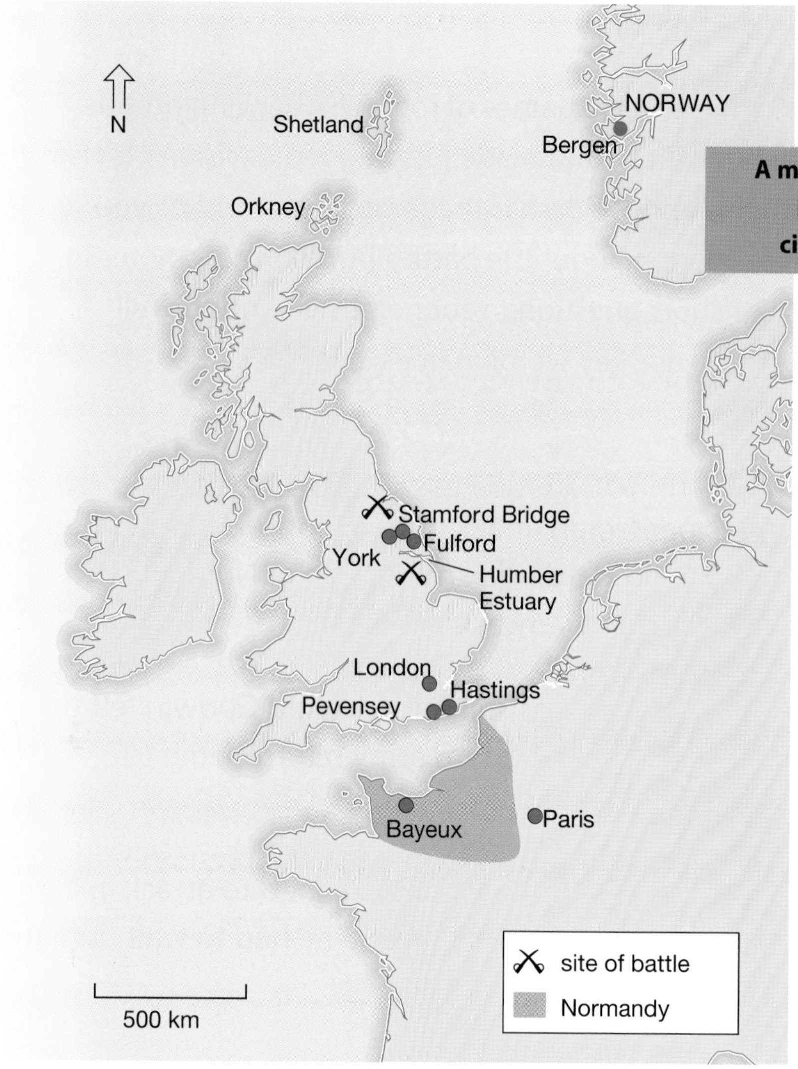
N
Shetland
Orkney
NORWAY
Bergen
Stamford Bridge
Fulford
York
Humber
Estuary
London
Hastings
Pevensey
Bayeux
Paris
site of battle
Normandy
500 km

A map of north-western Europe showing key cities and battle sites.

The Battle of Fulford Gate, 20 September 1066

At the end of August 1066, Harald Hardrada and his men left in Norway. Towns and villages along the east coast of Scotland and England were attacked and raided. Unfortunately for Hardrada, spies told Harold Godwin about these attacks.

Hardrada's army began marching towards York. About one kilometre from York, an English army led by Edwin of Mercia and Morcar of Northumbria lay in wait at Fulford Gate. On 20 September, a 30-minute fight ended in victory for Hardrada.

Four days later (24 September), York surrendered to Harald Hardrada without a fight. But Hardrada did not know that Harold Godwin and his men were on their way north to deal with the invaders.

- 💡 Why do you think Hardrada's men raided coastal towns and villages?
- 💡 What advantage do you think these attacks gave Harold Godwin?
- 💡 How do you think Hardrada felt after the victories at Fulford Gate and York?

The Battle of Stamford Bridge, 25 September 1066

Harald Hardrada ordered the people of York to hand over supplies to his men at a place called Stamford Bridge. On 25 September, Hardrada and one-third of his men set off to collect the goods. Tostig was among this group of soldiers. Hardrada ordered them to leave their armour on board the ships and carry only swords.

As Hardrada and his men began collecting their supplies, Harold Godwin's army suddenly arrived. Hardrada had not expected Godwin's army to get there so quickly.

Harold Godwin tried to get his brother Tostig to change sides and fight for him. But Tostig would not accept Harold's offer of a **pardon**. Harold returned to his men and the battle began. By late afternoon, Tostig had been slaughtered and Hardrada had been killed by an arrow to his throat.

Key words

Pardon An official statement of forgiveness.

A modern painting of the Battle of Stamford Bridge in 1066.

Hardrada's soldiers were also killed. But the rest of the Viking army had arrived. The exhausted English army was then forced to fight for another three or four hours before the Vikings were finally defeated.

- Why do you think Hardrada took so few men to Stamford Bridge?

- What do you think we can learn about Hardrada from this decision?

- How do you think Harald Hardrada's men helped William?

TASKS...

1 Write a newspaper headline about the Battle of Stamford Bridge. Your headline must state who won and who lost the battle, and give reasons why.

The Battle of Hastings, 14 October 1066

The morning after the Battle of Stamford Bridge, Harold tried to think about what to do next. No one knew if William had already landed in southern England.

Three decisions

Harold made three decisions. These would have a huge effect on the history of England.

ONE	TWO	THREE
He told his fyrd army that they would not receive any wages until William had been beaten as well.	He employed a man called Meruleswegen to rule northern England, instead of leaving the job to the earls.	He decided to ride as fast as he could to the south coast. He ordered the fyrd and his archers to rest for two days, then meet him near London.

TASKS...

1 In pairs, look at Harold's three decisions. *Think very hard* about what might have happened after each decision. List one or two *good* things and one or two *bad* things about each decision. For example, for decision One, a good thing might be that the army would fight hard so that they would get the gold. A bad thing for decision One might be that the army may decide to run away and not fight.

2 What advice would you have given Harold about his three decisions? Discuss your ideas with a partner.

Tactics

On 26 September 1066, Harold and his soldiers began their week-long ride towards London. William and his men set sail from Normandy and landed near Pevensey on the south coast on 28 September. To William's relief, the area was completely undefended. Harold had wrongly guessed that William would invade Dover.

William ordered a castle to be built in Pevensey. He then attacked English farms, stealing animals and burning down homes.

On 6 October, Harold Godwin arrived in London. He already knew about William's arrival. Harold had to think again about what to do next. He had two options.

OPTION 1:
I could attack William immediately.

OPTION 2:
I could attack William later.

This tactic had defeated Hardrada just two weeks earlier, so it seemed a sensible plan. But Harold's fyrd had not come back from Stamford Bridge yet, so he would need to call a brand new fyrd.

Harold's younger brother Gyrth suggested this idea. He said Harold should wait for the fyrd and archers to arrive, then make preparations for the attack on William. By doing this, they would have a much larger army than the Normans.

💡 What would you have done if you were Harold?

💡 What do you think William was hoping Harold would decide?

The attack

In the end, Harold decided on Option 1 – to attack immediately. He called together a fyrd army from the counties of southern England. The brand new army had to march from London towards Hastings in just three days. Unlike Hardrada, William had positioned watchmen who told him of Harold's midnight arrival.

TASKS...

1 Imagine you are one of Harold's soldiers. Normally, their wives watch them in battle from a nearby hill and bury them if they die. But your wife can't come this time. Tell her all about the last few weeks.

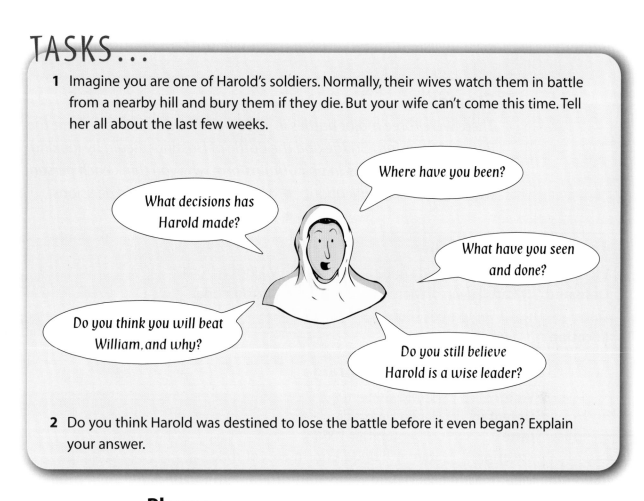

Where have you been?

What decisions has Harold made?

What have you seen and done?

Do you think you will beat William, and why?

Do you still believe Harold is a wise leader?

2 Do you think Harold was destined to lose the battle before it even began? Explain your answer.

Plenary

List three things that were important in deciding what happened at the battles of Fulford Gate and Stamford Bridge.

Now write down what you think was the most important thing for each battle. Give reasons for your choice.

DID HAROLD DESERVE TO LOSE THE ENGLISH THRONE?

By the end of this section you will be able to answer the key question:
• Did Harold deserve to be defeated at the Battle of Hastings?

You will also look at:
• how debate can help us to listen to other views and learn new ideas
• how you can persuade other people to change their opinions.

Starter

There were three major battles in 1066 – the Battle of Fulford Gate, the Battle of Stamford Bridge and the Battle of Hastings. Begin by looking at the first two battles. In pairs, brainstorm why you think each person won that battle. Think about: ● *good luck* ● *good decisions* ● *bad decisions.*

The Battle of Fulford Gate	
Victor	Harald Hardrada and the Norwegian Vikings
Defeated	Earls Edwin of Mercia and Morcar of Northumbria
Date	20 September 1066
Location	Fulford, near York

The Battle of Stamford Bridge	
Victor	Harold Godwin
Defeated	Harald Hardrada
Date	25 September 1066
Location	Stamford Bridge, north-east of York

For each battle, make a chart like the one below. Fill in as much information as you can. Look back at page 34 to see how you did this for the football match.

Good luck	Good decisions	Bad decisions

Defeat for Harold

The Battle of Hastings began on the morning of 14 October 1066. It lasted all day. The timeline, the map and Sources A to D record the key events of the battle.

TIMELINE
The Battle of Hastings, 14 October 1066

7 am Harold positions his soldiers at the top of Senlac Hill.

11 am William sends in his soldiers. They are quickly cut down by Harold's soldiers, who also holds up well against the Norman cavalry.

12.30 pm As some of the Norman cavalry retreat, a small number of the English fyrd chase after them. Had William now learned a way of drawing the English from their hill top position?

1.30 pm In the middle of a successful English attack on the Normans, Harold's brother, Leofwine, is killed. Harold orders his men to return to the top of Senlac Hill.

Thirty minutes later, Harold's brother, Gyrth, is killed.

4.30 pm William's cavalry successfully attacks the fyrd on Harold's right side. Many of the fyrd are scared and run away. The English are soon outnumbered and the Normans get closer.

5.15 pm The soldiers form a defensive wall around Harold. One by one they die, until Harold too is killed. Not a single soldier is left alive by nightfall.

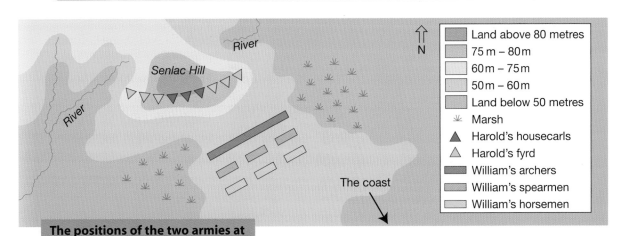

Land above 80 metres
75 m – 80 m
60 m – 75 m
50 m – 60 m
Land below 50 metres
Marsh
Harold's housecarls
Harold's fyrd
William's archers
William's spearmen
William's horsemen

The positions of the two armies at the Battle of Hastings.

SOURCE A

Our soldiers attacked the English. The English fought back bravely with spears, axes and stones. The English stayed on high ground and pushed our knights down the hill.

Our knights remembered about pretending to retreat. Several thousand English soldiers followed them down the hill. The Normans suddenly turned their horses, surrounded the English and cut them down. The Normans played this trick twice, and at last the English were defeated.

From a description by William of Poitiers. He was a Norman who was not at the battle but was one of William's most trusted officials.

SOURCE B

William took Harold by surprise before his men were ready to fight. The English army had a very small space. Many soldiers deserted Harold when they saw this difficult position. Even so, Harold fought bravely. William's army did not have much effect. After a lot of killing on both sides, the king fell.

An extract from the Anglo-Saxon Chronicle, written by English monks. This recorded the English view of what happened at the Battle of Hastings.

SOURCE C

A scene from the Bayeux Tapestry. It shows Harold being killed (by an arrow in the eye). The Bayeux Tapestry tells the whole story of the Norman conquest of England.

SOURCE D

The first knight pierced Harold's shield and then his chest, drenching the ground with his blood which poured out.

With his sword, the second knight cut off Harold's head. The third knight attacked him with his spear.

The fourth knight hacked off his leg at the thigh and threw it away.

Harold's dead body lay on the ground.

An extract from a poem written in about 1068 by a Norman bishop.

By the evening, Harold and his army had been completely destroyed by the Normans. On 25 December 1066, William of Normandy was crowned King of England in London.

TASKS...

1 In groups, answer the following questions.

   (a) Do you think William would have won if Harold had more archers and reinforcements?

   (b) Why do you think that Sources A to D give different versions of what happened at the Battle of Hastings?

2 Now try to decide why the Battle of Hastings ended as it did. Fill in the chart below to show the good luck and good decisions for William, and the bad decisions for Harold. In pairs, brainstorm why William won the battle.

Good luck	Good decisions	Bad decisions

3 Now that you have come to the end of your investigation, you must reach some conclusions. Start with a revision game to see how much information you can remember. Look at the chart below. For each of the six rows, work out which person, thing or event is the odd one out. Share your views with a neighbour, then with the whole class.

1	King Edward	Prince Edgar	Harold Godwin	Harald Hardrada	William of Normandy
2	Harthacanute	William of Normandy	Emma	Ethelred	Harefoot
3	slingshot	canons	bow and arrow	warhorses	axes
4	York	Stamford Bridge	Hastings	Fulford	Pevensey
5	William of Normandy	Harold Godwin	Edward the Confessor	Harald Hardrada	Tostig
6	Romans	Nazis	Celts	Normans	Vikings

4 As a class, debate the question: *'Did Harold deserve to lose the English throne?'* A good debate on this should tackle the following questions. **WS**

- *Whose claim to the throne was the greater – Harold's or William's?*

- *Whose army was more powerful – Harold's or William's?*

- *Who made the best and worst decisions – Harold or William?*

- *Who was luckier – Harold or William?*

Plenary

History is all about what happened in the past. But sometimes it can be useful to think about some 'What if ...?' questions. As a class, discuss the questions below. See if you can add any more 'What if ...?' questions to this list.

- *What if* Hardrada had not bothered to invade England?

- *What if* Harold had accepted William as king, and William fought Hardrada instead?

- *What if* Harold had escaped the battlefield at Hastings?

- *What if* Hardrada had won the Battle of Stamford Bridge?

- *What if* William's navy had been sunk by Harold's navy?

We can't change History! But we can use 'What if ...?' questions to think about the effects of minor decisions or events. Today England would be a very different place if Harald Hardrada or Harold Godwin had won. Try to list one decision Harold Godwin and Harald Hardrada should have made that might have led to their victory in 1066.

DID WILLIAM'S CONQUEST CHANGE ENGLAND?

William was a Frenchman who had just become King of England. What problems do you think he would face as a king in a strange country? Try to think of three.

Now put these problems in order, starting with the most serious at the top and ending with the least serious at the bottom.

Try to say how you would solve these problems if you had been William in 1066.

TIMELINE

1066 Harold Godwin dies. William of Normandy is named King of England.

1070 William has defeated his enemies in Kent, Exeter, Durham and York.

1072 Scotland surrenders to William.

1075 William defeats his enemies in East Anglia and Hereford.

1080 Nearly all of the English bishops in the Church are replaced by French bishops.

1086 The 'Domesday Survey' is done.

1087 William dies in France.

What happened after 1066?

In Chapter 1, you found out how William beat the English. You also learned how Harold Godwin died in 1066.

This chapter looks at the years after 1066. William was French. He gave lots of English land to the Frenchmen who had helped him to beat Harold. He also set up the feudal system, which told people what rights they had and what duties they had to do. He built castles and cathedrals all over the country. He made changes to church buildings and services.

Historians disagree about these changes. Some say that in 1066 everything changed forever. Others say there wasn't that much change at all.

Just how much do you think the Norman invasion changed life in England? When you have read this chapter, you should be able to make up your own mind.

HOW IMPORTANT WAS HAROLD'S DEATH?

Objectives

By the end of this section you will be able to answer these questions.

- What did people think about Harold's death?

- What questions might English people want to ask about their new king?

Starter

Imagine it is a few days after the Battle of Hastings. You are an Englishman, and you are drinking with some friends in a tavern (an inn where you can buy and drink alcohol). A trader, who is also drinking in the tavern, says he was at Hastings the morning after the battle had ended. He tells you a story. When you have heard the whole story, you will find clues to show that the trader was on Harold's side and that he did not like William. **WS**

- *Work in pairs. Pick out all the words and phrases in the trader's story that show he was on Harold's side.*

- *What questions would you like to ask the trader? Come up with at least two.*

Now find someone else in the class who has two different questions. Explain to each other why you chose your questions.

What the trader said

It was a cold autumn morning. Everywhere I looked I saw dead soldiers covered in blood. Their faces showed the pain they had gone through when they had bravely tried to save our king. I began to think about our defeat. Would we now be slaves to William? I helped people to search for their relatives. It was a terrible job.

A few hours before, these men had stood bravely on Senlac Hill. They had put their shields together to form a wall. This defended them from the Norman attacks. Harold – our leader and king – tried to stop the invasion by the evil Norman duke, William of Normandy. But his plans had gone wrong.

Our brave men had held the Normans back all day. But just when the Norman soldiers looked tired, Harold was hit by an arrow. It went straight through his eye and into his brain. His bodyguards tried to help him, but they were too late. The Normans charged again. This time, Harold was trapped. They chopped his body into pieces. The battle was over.

'Here! He lies here!' shouted one of the women helping to look for Harold. They recognised his body because of his tattoos. I tell you, these are bad times. What can we expect now that we are to be ruled by a foreign king?

TASKS...

1 Make a list of any *new* things you have found out about the Norman Conquest.

2 Some historians think the Norman invasion was a turning point in English history. Do you agree? Write down three reasons to explain your answer. When you have finished Chapter 2, check your three reasons again and see whether there is anything you would like to change.

Plenary

Imagine you are one of Harold's relatives who found his dead body in 1066. How would you want the English people to remember him?

Write about 20 words that could be carved on Harold's gravestone to tell people what he was like.

HOW MUCH DID THE ENGLISH TRY TO STOP THE NORMAN INVASION?

Objectives

By the end of this section you will be able to answer these questions.

- How long did it take William to beat all those people who did not want him to be king?

- How did William deal with people who opposed him?

Starter

Look at Source A. Now look at the word grid below it. Pick out the words you think describe the way the people in Source A must have been feeling at the time.

SOURCE A

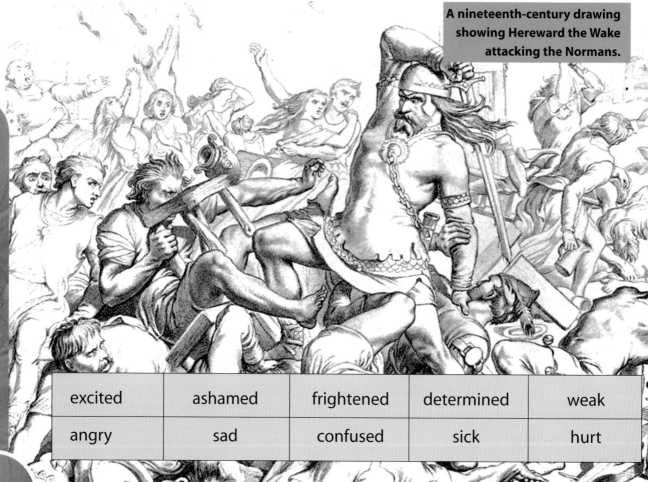

A nineteenth-century drawing showing Hereward the Wake attacking the Normans.

excited	ashamed	frightened	determined	weak
angry	sad	confused	sick	hurt

Look at Source A again. Imagine you are the man wearing the helmet in the middle of the picture. Describe who you are and what you are doing. Why are you attacking the people in the picture?

💡 *Why do you think Hereward was called 'the Wake'?*

💡 *What do you think this tells us about him?*

The rebellion of Hereward the Wake

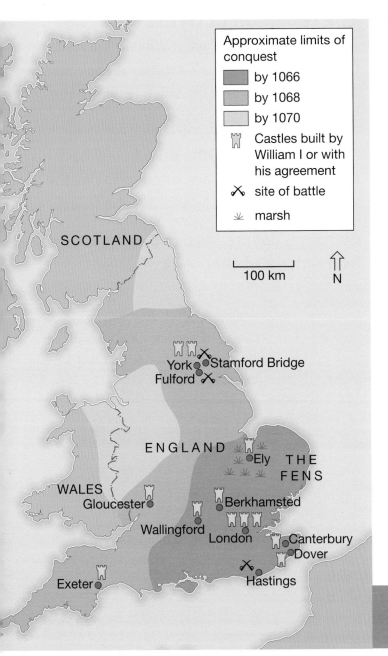

Approximate limits of conquest

▨	by 1066
▨	by 1068
▨	by 1070

🏰 Castles built by William I or with his agreement

✕ site of battle

�’ marsh

SCOTLAND

100 km

⇧ N

York 🏰🏰 ✕ Stamford Bridge
Fulford ✕

ENGLAND 🏰 ⚒ Ely   THE
⚒ ⚒ ⚒   FENS

WALES 🏰
Gloucester ● 🏰 Berkhamsted
Wallingford 🏰🏰🏰
London ● 🏰 Canterbury
🏰 Dover
✕
Exeter ● 🏰 Hastings

The man in the centre of Source A is Hereward the Wake. In 1070, Hereward rebelled against the new king, William. Other people before Hereward had tried to remove William. Hereward joined with Edwin (the Earl of Mercia), Morcar (the Earl of Northumberland) and an army from Denmark. He managed to keep the Normans out of Ely for a year, but he was eventually defeated.

A map showing William's control over different parts of Britain at different times in his reign.

There are many stories about Hereward the Wake. They tell of his strength and fighting skill. Source A was drawn in the nineteenth century. It shows Hereward taking revenge on some Normans, who had broken into his home. At another time Hereward visited William's court disguised as a potter, when some drunken servants attacked him. Read Source B to find out what happened.

Snatching a piece of wood from the fireplace, Hereward defended himself against them all. He killed one of them and wounded many. He was taken prisoner, but managed to escape back to Ely. He captured a Norman who had chased after him. Hereward sent him back to William to tell the Normans the truth about what had happened. Everybody said that Hereward was a generous and remarkable knight.

From *Gesta Herewardi*, written by a monk in the twelfth century. It is based on stories passed on by eyewitnesses.

The rebellion of Gytha

Another rebellion against William was led by Gytha, Harold Godwin's mother. It took place in 1068 in Exeter (Devon), which is where the Godwin family had a home.

After Harold died, Gytha tried to buy back his body from King William, offering to pay the weight of the body in gold. But she failed.

Gytha was not prepared to give in to the new king without a fight.

 SOURCE C

In 1068, the people of Exeter would not let King William into their city. So he blockaded the city walls, which meant no one could get in or out.

One rebel stood on the castle wall, bared his bottom and broke wind in front of the Normans! William was furious. He took hostages and had them blinded.

After eighteen days, Exeter was forced to surrender when William managed to get in to the city.

Gytha managed to escape, taking with her a great store of treasure. Eventually, she returned to Denmark. The resistance of the Godwin family was over.

An account of Gytha's rebellion, based on eyewitness stories.

TASKS...

1 **(a)** Look at the map on page 51. It suggests that, by 1066, William controlled the eastern Fens. Do you think this is true?

(b) The map suggests that, by 1070, William controlled most of England. Do you think this is true? Give reasons for your answers.

2 Look at Source A. Do you think the artist liked Hereward or not? Use details from the source to support your answer.

3 Read Source B. Do you think this story could be true? Give reasons for your answer.

4 Read Source C. What do you think Gytha would have written in her diary about the rebellion? Write her version of what happened. **WS**

Plenary

Look again at Sources B and C. Why do you think it was important for English people to have stories like these after William's invasion. Discuss as a class.

HOW DID WILLIAM TAKE CONTROL OF THE REST OF THE COUNTRY?

Objectives

By the end of this section you will be able to answer these questions.
- How much did English people resist the Normans?
- How quickly did William gain control of England?

You will use sources to help you answer these questions.

Starter

Imagine you are William's top adviser. It is 1070 and William is keen to return to Normandy. He wants to spend some time with his friends and family. He wants to know whether he can leave England in the hands of his supporters without the English overthrowing him when he has gone. Write a paragraph to William giving your opinion on whether it is safe for him to leave at this time. Think about everything that has happened between 1066 and 1070 before you write your advice. Be prepared to share your opinion with others in the class.

Opposition to William

William had to deal with lots of opposition after 1066. He had to fight for several years to gain control over England. Historians do not agree on how quickly William managed to get this control. Read Source A and pick out three ways in which William managed to gain control. You could make this a spider diagram.

How quickly did William gain control?

Look at Sources B to E. As you will see, historians have different views about how quickly William managed to take control of England. Think carefully about your own views as you read the sources. Then do the tasks.

1066 • William marches to London killing many English people on his way.
• Three important English **nobles** surrender.
• William is crowned King of England.

1067 • William defeats his enemies in Kent.

1068 • The people of Exeter resist William for eighteen days.
• William kills hundreds of rebels in Durham and sets the town on fire.

1069 • William's castle in York is burnt down and Norman soldiers are killed.
• William retakes York by force.
• All crops, herds, flocks and food north of the River Humber are burnt and destroyed.
• About 100,000 people die in the famine. (This becomes known as 'The Harrying of the North'.)

1070 • Rising led by Hereward the Wake.
• It is eventually defeated one year later.
• Hereward escapes.

1072 • Rising by the Scots.
• They surrender as soon as William sends in his armies.

1075 • Risings in East Anglia and Hereford.
• William defeats both sets of enemies.

1080 • Norman bishop of Durham and 100 supporters are murdered by rebels in Northumberland.

1086 • Prince Edgar leads a revolt with help from the Danes.
• The revolt fails.

1087 • Death of William.

A list of events from various reports written by twelfth-century monks.

Key words

Noble A rich and powerful member of an important family.

By spring 1070, William was in control. Although there were other rebellions, they were not as serious as the rebellions of 1067 and 1069.

A modern historian writing in a textbook in 2000.

Many historians think that the English stopped resisting the Normans after they lost the Battle of Hastings. This is not true. From 1066 up to 1086 the English kept on resisting.

From an article on the Internet about 1066.

TASKS...

1 Draw a table in your books like the one below.

Date	William's actions	English resistance

Fill in the chart using details from the timeline on page 55.

2 Working in pairs, decide whether the statements below are true or false. Explain why.

a) William only took strong action against the English when they strongly resisted him.

b) William's actions against the English got stronger as the years went by.

c) William was resisted by the English everywhere he went.

d) Most of the English resistance to William came after 1075.

3 How long did it take William to get control? Look at each source and decide when each one suggests that William had control.

EXTENSION TASK...

4 Design a poster about 'The Harrying of the North' to show the people of Britain the truth about William's cruelty. Design your poster from an English point of view.

Plenary

By which date do you think William was in control of England?

● 1070　　● 1072　　● 1075　　● 1080　　● 1087

Explain your answers.

THE FEUDAL SYSTEM: A WORLD TURNED UPSIDE DOWN?

By the end of this section you will be able to answer these questions.

• What was the feudal system?

• Was this system completely new after 1066?

Starter

Look at Sources A and B. Both pictures come from manuscripts that show scenes from life in the Middle Ages. They show the king with some of his people.

SOURCE A

A twelfth-century painting of William with Alan of Brittany.

SOURCE B

A twelfth-century picture of a noble with the king.

💡 *In each picture, who do you think is in control?*

💡 *Why do you think the knights are standing behind the king in Source A?*

💡 *In Source A, there is another person in the picture. Who do you think this person is?*

💡 *What do you think Sources A and B tell us about the relationship between the king and the people in the Middle Ages?*

What was England like before 1066?

Look at the diagram below, which shows the way English people were organised before 1066.

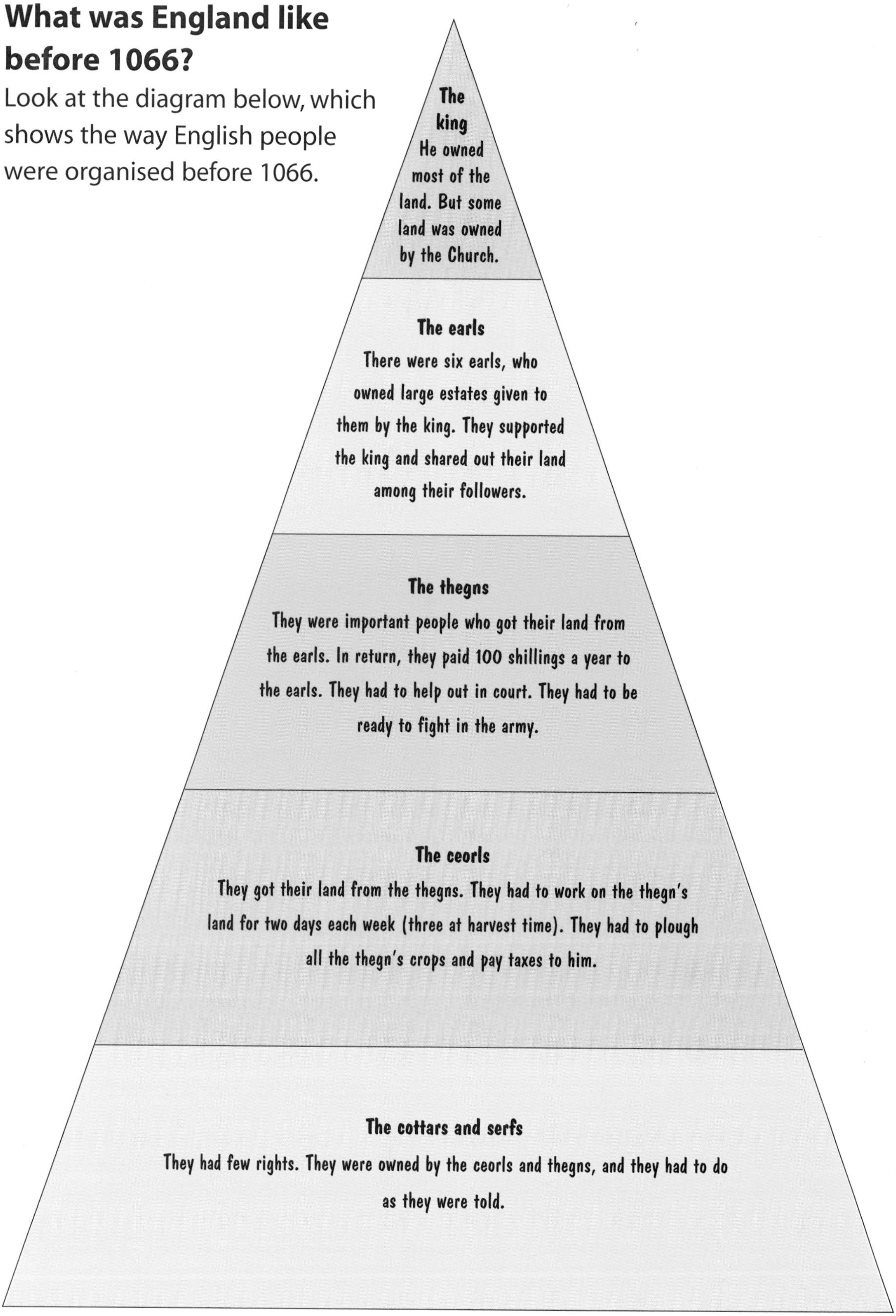

The king
He owned most of the land. But some land was owned by the Church.

The earls
There were six earls, who owned large estates given to them by the king. They supported the king and shared out their land among their followers.

The thegns
They were important people who got their land from the earls. In return, they paid 100 shillings a year to the earls. They had to help out in court. They had to be ready to fight in the army.

The ceorls
They got their land from the thegns. They had to work on the thegn's land for two days each week (three at harvest time). They had to plough all the thegn's crops and pay taxes to him.

The cottars and serfs
They had few rights. They were owned by the ceorls and thegns, and they had to do as they were told.

The feudal system after 1066

The king

William kept one-fifth of the land in England for his own royal estates. He gave one-quarter of the rest to the Church. What was left was shared between 180 of his followers.

The barons

These followers were barons. They became known as tenants-in-chief. In return for their land they promised to obey William and give his army money or soldiers. They kept some land for themselves and split up the rest into manors, which they gave to their followers.

The knights

These men were knights, who became known as under-tenants. In return for their land, they promised to obey the baron and serve as a knight in the army. They kept some land for themselves and shared the rest between the peasants, who lived on their manor.

The villeins

The peasants were called villeins. In return for their land, they had to obey the lord of the manor and give him part of their crops. They also worked without pay on the lord's land. Villeins had no freedom – they could not leave the lord's land without his permission. They even needed permission for their sons and daughters to get married!

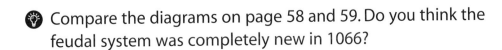
Compare the diagrams on page 58 and 59. Do you think the feudal system was completely new in 1066?

DID WILLIAM'S CONQUEST CHANGE ENGLAND?

How the feudal system worked

William owned all the land in England. But he could not manage it on his own. Also, he wanted to reward those supporters who had helped him beat Harold in the Battle of Hastings. So he shared the land with his supporters.

William lent large areas of land to powerful barons. They gave smaller areas of this land, called manors, to knights. Knights were soldiers who did not know much about farming. So they shared their manors among the peasants, or villeins, who worked on it.

This was called the feudal system. Each person made promises in return for their land. The diagram on page 59 shows the promises that each person made so they could hold onto their land. It also shows how the different groups in society were arranged.

SOURCE C

In 1086, there were still a few English landholders. They were not as rich or powerful as they had been in the past. They often got married to Normans. They still lived their lives as they had done before, so English customs and traditions carried on.

An historian writing in 1995.

How did the feudal system change England?

In 1086, William ordered a survey to show who owned each piece of land and how much money it was worth. This was called the 'Domesday Survey'. It showed that only two of the tenants-in-chief were English. The rest were Norman. The English earls and thegns had lost their land. It seemed like a lot had changed since 1066. But how big were these changes? Look at sources C to F.

SOURCE D

Knight service was new in the feudal system. Knights were important soldiers who fought on horseback.

An historian writing in 1968.

SOURCE E

People talk about the 'newness' of the feudal system. They say that holding land in return for service in the army was new. But even before 1066, landholders had to serve in the army. Although everything seemed to have changed after 1066, in many ways it was just the same.

Adapted from an article on the Internet.

SOURCE F

The Normans didn't change the systems of farming. People still wore the same kinds of clothing and lived in the same types of houses as they did before the Norman Conquest. The new Norman king and his lords were not interested in changing the ways ordinary people lived their lives.

The feudal system was a simple way of organising society. There were four main levels, or ranks (see page 59). Each had its own set of rights and duties. Today, society is much more complicated.

An historian writing in 2002.

TASKS...

1 Think of six people in today's society – for example, teacher, doctor, factory worker. Put who you think is the most important at the top of a list. Then place the rest in order underneath, until you reach who you think is the least important. Compare your list with others in your class.

DID WILLIAM'S CONQUEST CHANGE ENGLAND?

TASKS...

2 (a) Copy a chart like this one into your book. Use details from pages 58–61 to fill in the chart.

	Before 1066	After 1066
Who owned the land?		
Did military service exist?		
Who did military service?		
What was life like for ordinary people?		

(b) Get into groups to prepare a report on the question:
How 'new' was the feudal system?

Plenary

What were the main differences between the way England was organised before 1066, and after?

HOW FAR DID WILLIAM CHANGE THE ENGLISH CHURCH?

Objectives

By the end of this section you will be able to answer these questions.

• How important was the Church in the Middle Ages?

• What changes did William make to the English Church?

Starter

What do you know about religious buildings? How often do you visit one? In groups, draw a mind map about 'places of worship'. Include details of:

- *different types of places of worship*
- *the people who work there*
- *the different services that are held there*
- *whether a place of worship is important in your everyday life.*

The importance of the Church

In the Middle Ages, the Church played a very important part in peoples' lives. Look at the diagram on page 64. It shows how the Church was organised and how it helped people.

Ordinary people and the Church

In the Middle Ages, people went to **church** regularly. Church services were in Latin. Most ordinary people couldn't understand Latin. They couldn't read or write, either. Instead, they learned from listening to the priest or by looking at the wall paintings. These often showed frightening pictures of what it was like in hell.

To avoid going to hell, people had to admit their sins to the local priest. This was to show they were sorry. The priest also married people in church, baptised their babies and forgave the sins of people who were dying. So the priest was one of the most important men in the village.

The **Church** had a big influence on people. It told them that if they were bad, they would go to hell when they died. If they were good, they would go to heaven. Any king who could control the Church could also control the people.

Key words

church When a small 'c' is used, it means a local, or parish, church.

Church For this period when a capital 'C' is used, it refers to the whole of the Catholic Church led by the Pope.

💡 How do you think controlling the Church helped William to control the country?

The Pope.
• Head of the Catholic Church in all of Western Europe.
• All kings, princes and emperors obeyed him.

▼

💡 If you were William, how would you try to take control of the Church? You could brainstorm some ideas in pairs.

Bishops, Archbishops and Cardinals.
• Advised kings and emperors on how to govern their people.
• Became statesmen and diplomats.

Parish priest.
• Responsible for the parish church and his parishioners.
• Advised on spiritual matters.
• Taught the meaning of religion.
• Baptised, married and buried people.
• The parish church was a central place for community affairs, entertainment and socialising.

Monks and nuns.
• Worshipped privately in a monastery (monks) or a nunnery (nuns).
• Often conributed to the life of the community, caring for sick and poor people.
• Shut themselves away from the world in order to get closer to God.

Friars.
• Friars were travelling monks.
• They wandered from village to village, working and begging for food.
• They helped the sick in their homes, taught religious lessons, and carried news from village to village.

How William used his own men to work in the Church

First, William chose an abbot from Normandy to be the Archbishop of Canterbury. This was the most important job in the English Church, so William wanted to make sure the archbishop was loyal to him.

Then he gave large areas of land to bishops and abbots. He brought many new Church leaders to England from Normandy. In 1066, there were sixteen bishops in total, and all of them were English. By 1080, fifteen of the sixteen bishops were Normans. Most of the local priests were still English.

Changing Church customs and practices

The new Norman Church leaders began to introduce their own Church services. The abbot of Glastonbury made the monks sing Norman prayers. When the monks refused, the abbot sent for some knights. The knights broke down the abbey doors, killed three monks and wounded eighteen more. At Evesham, the bones of English saints were set on fire. At Ely, the church treasures were taken by William.

The Church calendar listed all the important religious events of the year. It was changed by the bishops. The priests were given new strict rules. These rules said they could no longer get married. They should dress in simple clothes, have their hair cut and rounded so that their ears could be seen, and stay out of inns and taverns.

💡 What effect do you think these changes had on the Church?

Building new churches

William built new churches and cathedrals. English churches were quite small and made of wood. Norman churches were larger and made of stone. The map on this page shows the new cathedrals built by the Normans. The photograph on page 66 shows Winchester Cathedral, begun in 1079.

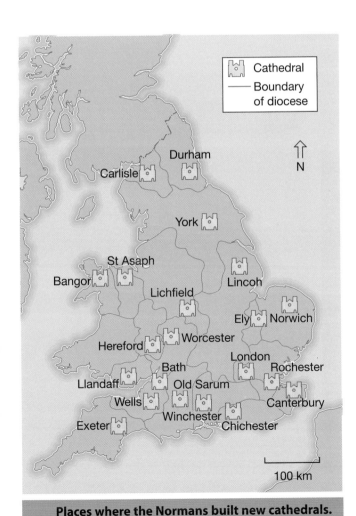

	Cathedral
—	Boundary of diocese

Durham
Carlisle
⇧ N
York
St Asaph
Bangor
Lincoh
Lichfield
Ely Norwich
Worcester
Hereford
London
Bath Rochester
Llandaff Old Sarum
Wells Canterbury
Exeter Winchester
Chichester

100 km

Places where the Normans built new cathedrals.

SOURCE A

An aerial view of Winchester Cathedral.

💡 Using Sources B and C, list the differences between English and Norman churches.

SOURCE B

A small English church built in the ninth century in Essex. The church is made from wood.

SOURCE C

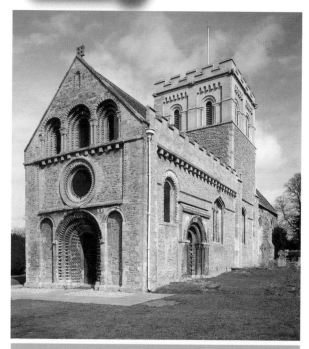

A church rebuilt by the Normans in Iffley, (Oxford), in the twelfth century.

TASKS...

1 Do you think William's changes improved the Church or not? Find evidence from pages 63–6 to show:
   (a) how the Church improved
   (b) how the Church stayed the same or even got worse.

EXTENSION TASK ...

2 Imagine you are a priest in 1087. Write a letter to your local tenant-in-chief complaining about the changes William has made to the Church. Now that William is dead, you think it is time to change some things back again. The guidelines below will help you. **WS**

What your letter is for

- To argue that William's changes have been bad for the Church.

- To make the tenant-in-chief ask the new king to bring back some of the old ways of the Church.

The sentence level

- Write your letter in the first person (for example, I, we).

- After your first three statements, use short sentences to emphasise everything that has gone wrong in the Church.

- Use words and phrases to explain your reasons – like this shows, because, therefore and in fact.

The text level

- Use different sizes of print and fonts to emphasise your points.

- Start with three statements about how the Church has 'fallen into bad ways' since William has been king. Back up each statement with evidence. End by saying that, unless things go back to how they were before William's arrival in England, the future looks bad.

- Use pictures to show the bad state of the English Church.

The word level

- Use words that will persuade the tenant-in-chief – such as clearly, necessary, scandal, criminal, the work of the devil.

- Choose words for their emotional effect and impact on the tenant-in-chief.

HOW DID CASTLES CHANGE THE ENGLISH LANDSCAPE?

Objectives

By the end of this section you will be able to answer these questions.

- What were the first Norman castles like?
- Where did William the Conqueror build castles?
- How did the castles affect English people between 1066 and 1087?

You will also be asked to:

- write a report
- use sources to investigate the effects of castles.

Starter

Have you ever seen a castle? What does a castle look like? From memory, draw a picture of a castle and label as many different parts of it as you can. Compare your castle with castles drawn by other classmates. Talk about how they are similar and different.

William's network of castles

Key words

Strategic Carefully chosen. You often use this word if you are talking about military plans.

Look at Source A on page 69. It shows a Norman castle.

William spent a long time trying to gain control of his new kingdom. He built a network of castles, like the one in Source A, at places known as **strategic** points. Later, you will discover how many castles William built after 1066.

Typical features of early Norman castles

- The castle builders first built up a mound of earth, called a motte.
- Around the bottom of this was a deep ditch.
- On top of the motte they built a wooden wall called a stockade, or a palisade.
- Inside the stockade they added a wooden tower, called a keep.

Key words

Drawbridge A bridge that can be raised or lowered to stop people getting in or out.

- Next to the motte was a yard, called a bailey. This was where the soldiers lived.
- If the castle was attacked, the soldiers would go to the keep across a wooden **drawbridge**.

SOURCE A

A typical Norman castle built after 1066.

TASKS...

1 Imagine you are building a castle. What kind of place would make a strategic point? Think about places that your enemy would find difficult to attack.

2 In pairs, brainstorm how you would attack a motte and bailey castle in Norman times.

3 How would you make this castle stronger?
- Make a list of the changes to the castle that you could make.
- Draw a new version of the castle showing all your changes.
- Label all the new features clearly.

DID WILLIAM'S CONQUEST CHANGE ENGLAND?

How did castles affect life in England after 1066?

TASKS ...

1 Working in groups, look at Sources B to E. Imagine you were living in England in the Norman period. Would you think that castles were a good or bad idea?

2 Study the sources and information carefully.

(a) In your book, write the heading 'Castles make life better for English people'. On another page, write the heading 'Castles make life worse for the English people'. Using details from the sources, make notes under each heading. **WS**

(b) When your notes are finished, discuss whether you think castles were good or bad for English people. **WS**

SOURCE B

The English had to get used to the castles and troops of heavily armed Norman knights. These men were their new lords. They spoke a different language and they had a lot of power over them.

An extract from a modern school textbook written in 2002.

English peasants, who have been turned out of their houses by the Normans. The peasants are forced to build a castle where their homes used to be.

SOURCE C

Some English people may have been grateful for castles. The areas around them were peaceful. Each castle provided work for skilled English craftsmen who brought their families to live near to the castle walls. Huts and houses would be built, and soon towns began to develop in these places.

An historian writing in 1997.

SOURCE D

The Normans knocked down houses to make way for new castles. Families who lost their homes had to look after themselves. They had to work as slaves to build the new castles.

An extract from a book written in 1985.

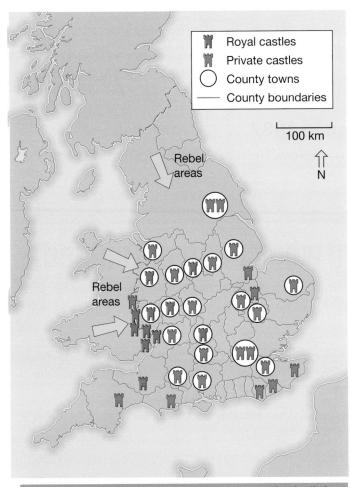

Royal castles
Private castles
County towns
County boundaries

100 km

N

Rebel areas

Rebel areas

The royal and private castles built by William the Conqueror.

SOURCE E

Castles were not new. Some Normans had already built castles in Herefordshire, Essex and Dover before 1066. The armies in the castles were often made up of Norman and English soldiers. English people were often given important jobs in the castle, like collecting taxes from local people and working in the law courts. Eventually, English people married Norman people.

From a textbook about the Normans written in 2002.

Plenary

Imagine it is 1087. News has just reached England that William has died. Using what you have learned so far in this chapter, write a paragraph to say how you feel about William's death. You can be either English or French.

DID WILLIAM'S CONQUEST CHANGE ENGLAND?

HOW DID WILLIAM'S CONQUEST CHANGE ENGLAND?

Objectives

By the end of this section you will be able to answer these questions.

- Was England in 1087 totally different from England in 1066?
- Were English people better off or worse off from the changes made by William?

Starter

Look back at the story told by the trader in the tavern at the beginning of this chapter (see pages 48-9). In his story, he describes his fears for England now that William is king. Was he right to be afraid? Remember your paragraph that you wrote for Task 2 on page 49? Now that you have got to the end of the chapter, do you still agree with your answer?

William's reputation in 1087

Read the newspaper story below, then answer the questions that follow it.

The Daily Norman   1087

Shock death of king who changed England!

News has come from France that William is dead. He died in a tragic accident. He was thrown off his horse and injured in the stomach by his saddle.

William had many achievements. By 1070, he had got England under control and put a stop to all of the resistance to him, just four years after being crowned King of England. He built new castles everywhere in England, which totally changed people's lives. He replaced all the wooden churches with new stone ones, and he replaced all the old bishops and priests too, bringing new life to the Church.

William introduced the feudal system, which was completely new. This helped him to set up control.

Looking back over his reign, it is incredible to see what a difference he made. England today is totally different from 1066. May his soul rest in peace. Amen.

Key words

Biased When someone's opinion is influenced by personal feelings or a lack of information.

- Which words and phrases do you think show that the writer is on William's side?
- Who do you think might have written the story and why?
- Is the writer **biased**?

TASKS...

1   In 1087, was England totally different to England before 1066? Write an essay about how much William changed England. Think about these questions.

- What did the English think about their new king in 1066?
- How soon did William defeat his English opponents?
- Was the feudal system totally new?

- How far did William change the Church?
- How much did castles change England?

Give your conclusion to the key question: *'Did William's conquest change England?'*

Use the following guide to help you write your essay.

- Write a title.
- Write an introduction that sets out your aims.
- Put each new point in a separate paragraph.
- Start each paragraph with a topic sentence that introduces the point you are going to make.
- Support the argument in each paragraph by adding evidence from your reading.
- Use quotes from your reading.
- Write in the third person and past tense when you are describing events and changes.
- Write in the first person and the present tense when you are giving your personal views.
- Use connectives. For example:
    - when putting events in order, use next, then, first, second, third, finally
    - when comparing and contrasting, use in the same way, similarly, instead of, otherwise
    - when explaining the cause and effect of events, use because, so, therefore
    - when supporting your views with evidence, use for example, such as, for instance, as shown by.
- Write a conclusion that sets out your overall opinion about the question you were set. **WS**

EXTENSION TASK...

2 Create your own newspaper story about William's reign, written from an English point of view.

(a) Think about the type of newspaper you are writing for. Is it going to be a paper like the *Daily Mirror* or *The Times*? This will affect your writing style.

(b) Choose a good headline and use short, punchy sentences.

(c) Think carefully about the pictures you will use.

Plenary

You have learned a lot of new words in this chapter. You could play a word game like 'Word bingo' or 'Odd One Out' to test how much you have learned. **WS**

WAS MEDIEVAL MEDICINE ALL 'DOOM AND GLOOM'?

3

TIMELINE
The development of medicine, 1066–1500

1066 No one understands that germs cause disease, so people do not think it is important to be clean.

1096 Religious people start to go on Crusades to the Holy Land. When they return they bring back new ideas about medicine from Arab doctors.

1237 Pipes are laid to carry clean water from the countryside into London.

1272 A priest, Roger Bacon, is put in prison for saying that doctors should experiment with their own ideas and not use old methods.

1349 The Black Death plague spreads across Europe.

1400 The Christian Church says that medical schools can dissect (cut up) human bodies.

1448 The first printing presses mean that ideas about medicine spread widely.

In this chapter you will:

- *Look at ideas about medicine, health and hygiene in the Middle Ages.*

- *Find out what medieval people thought caused disease.*

- *Look at what it was like to give birth to children in the Middle Ages.*

- *Develop your own ideas about why medieval towns were in such a bad state.*

- *Produce a piece of writing to answer the question: 'Was medieval medicine all doom and gloom?'*

Look at this picture of a scene in the Middle Ages.

Parents mourn a young victim of the Black Death. It is thought that one in three people died from this plague.

💡 *Use the 5Ws (who, when, where, what and why?) to find out as much as you can from this picture.*

💡 *Share your questions with the class. Choose some of the best ones to display and see if the class can answer them over the next few lessons.*

WHAT WERE HOSPITALS LIKE AND HOW WERE THE SICK TREATED IN THEM?

Objectives

By the end of this section you will be able to answer these questions.

• What were hospitals and medical treatment like in the Middle Ages?

• How does this compare with what we have today?

Starter

Have you ever been in a hospital? What was it like?

In groups, brainstorm all the ideas you can think of about what it might be like inside a modern hospital. Write these down. Compare your ideas with another group. Add to your list any points that you missed.

Treatment of the sick

Modern hospitals might be scary places, but they are very different to the places where people were treated in the Middle Ages.

Key words

Leprosy A disease that causes terrible infections all over your body. People who get this disease are called lepers.

There were about 1200 hospitals in England and Wales in the Middle Ages, but they were not like hospitals today. They were run by monks and nuns. Some were just places for travellers to shelter. Some were to keep people who had **leprosy** away from the public. Half of them were places of rest for the old and poor. Only one out of every ten hospitals tried to help sick people get better.

Even so, some of these hospitals were quite big, with spaces for over 200 patients. Four hospitals were for pregnant women, and there was one hospital for the blind and deaf. Source A on page 78 shows nuns in a fifteenth-century hospital.

⚙ How different is the hospital in Source A from a modern hospital?

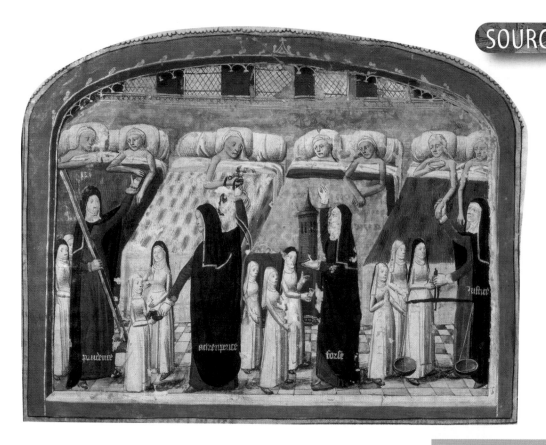

Christian nuns in a fifteenth-century hospital.

Operations

Only simple things like swellings, broken bones or injuries from war wounds were operated on. The surgeon had to work quickly to chop off the injured part, because the patient might die from pain or losing too much blood. Sometimes, patients were given a mixture made from **opium** and herbs to try to take away the pain. But this did not work very well.

Key words

Opium A drug made from poppies.

Barber-surgeons

For most people, operations were done in shops owned by 'barber-surgeons'. These were people who would cut hair and pull out teeth.

Blood letting When you cut the skin to make it bleed.

Barber-surgeons learned by watching other barber-surgeons. They thought that **blood letting** helped to cure people of illness. They did not wear special clothes and their equipment was dirty. On operating days, they hung their blood-stained towels outside on a white pole. Some modern barber shops still have a red and white pole outside.

Trained doctors did not like barber-surgeons because they had no qualifications. However, barber-surgeons were popular with ordinary people, who could not afford to pay doctors for treatment.

SOURCE B

The pole outside a modern-day barber's shop.

SOURCE C

An engraving from 1556 by Pieter Bruegel. His aim here was to make fun of the work of barber-surgeons.

WAS MEDIEVAL MEDICINE ALL 'DOOM AND GLOOM'?

TASKS...

1 Look at Sources A and C. Pick out some differences between medieval medicine and modern medicine. Produce a mind map to show:

The differences between medieval and modern hospitals and the treatment of the sick.

Your mind map might look something like this:

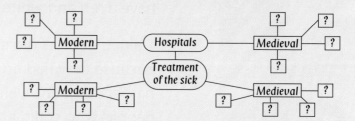

2 **(a)** In groups, study the sets of words in the grid below. These words help to describe hospitals and treatment during the Middle Ages.

You should know most of these words, but look up the meanings of any that you are unsure of.

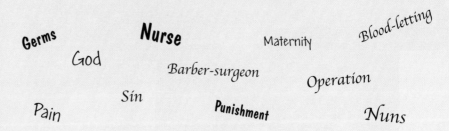

(b) Make two lists – one headed 'Medieval' and one headed 'Modern'. Now write each word in the correct list. If you think the word belongs in the 'Medieval' list, write it there. If you think it belongs in the 'Modern' list, write it there. If you can't decide, write it in both lists! **WS**

3 Now arrange these words under two *different* headings:
   - Good things about hospitals and treatment in the Middle Ages.
   - Bad things about hospitals and treatment in the Middle Ages.
   Make two lists, as you did for Task 2.

Plenary

Think of one piece of advice you would give to a barber-surgeon to help improve his patient survival rates.

HOW EFFECTIVE WERE MEDIEVAL DOCTORS?

Objectives

By the end of this section you will be able to answer these questions.

• What did people in the Middle Ages think about the causes of disease?

• How did doctors do their work?

Starter

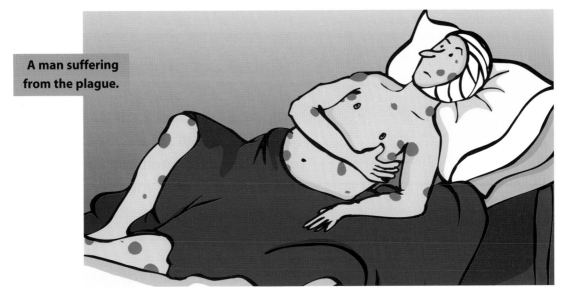

A man suffering from the plague.

Key words

Diagnosis   When a doctor identifies a disease based on its signs and symptoms.
Treatment   Care given by a doctor to relieve illness.

*Look at the drawing above. If this person visited a doctor today, what do you think would happen? In pairs, make a list of the things you would expect the doctor to do. Think about the doctor's **diagnosis** and **treatment**.*

TASKS...

1 In this activity, you will look at the work of doctors. **WS**
   • Your aim is to produce a number of slides or information cards with short notes and pictures.
   • You could produce these on card, poster paper, overhead projector transparencies or using a presentation package such as PowerPoint.
   • Make sure the work is shared out equally in your group.

TASKS...

You can use the information on the following pages, but you must pick out key points rather than copying material out! Try to use other resources to find extra information.

As preparation, divide a large piece of paper into four columns. Write the headings below at the top of the columns.

Causes of disease	Methods of diagnosis	Treatment of everyday illnesses	Development of knowledge and skills

Causes of disease

Doctors did not know that germs caused disease. They had some common-sense ideas and some superstitions about why diseases happened. Look at Sources A to D. They should give you four different views on what caused disease.

SOURCE A

God is terrible towards men. He often allows plagues, famines, wars and other forms of suffering to happen, and so the people of England are to be visited by the plague.

From a monk's letter to the Bishop of London, 1348.

SOURCE B

The cause of the plague was the close position of Saturn, Jupiter and Mars. Such a coming together of planets is always a sign of terrible or violent things to come.

Guy de Chauliac, a famous doctor writing in the 1300s.

SOURCE C

Doctors thought that the body was made up of four humours – earth, fire, water and air. If these humours got out of balance you would be ill. In summer, the heat would increase the fire so you would get very hot and bad tempered. In winter, the damp would increase the water, making you suffer from coughs and colds.

From a textbook published in 1991.

SOURCE D

In the Middle Ages, people thought that worms were connected to illness. When doctors examined the faeces of sick people, they often saw worms. They thought these had caused the illness.

From a textbook published in 1996.

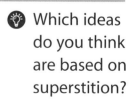

Which of the ideas in Sources A to D do you think are based on common sense?

Which ideas do you think are based on superstition?

Methods of diagnosis

Doctors trained for many years. They also read from Greek and Latin books. They thought it was important to be able to write and speak well, and have a good mind. They studied arithmetic, so that they could count the number of hours a patient had been suffering from pain. They believed that music was a great help to the sick. They also thought that knowing about **astronomy** would help them to find the cause of disease.

Doctors sometimes checked the pulse of the patient, and often looked at the patient's urine. A chart told them that if the urine was clear, the patient had good digestion. Black and cloudy urine meant the opposite, and could lead to death.

SOURCE E

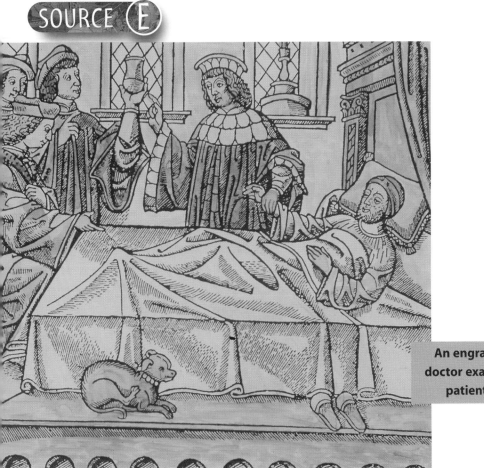

An engraving of a doctor examining a patient in 1345.

💡 What does this source tell you about medieval medical examinations?

The treatment of everyday illnesses

Doctors used herbal potions and mixtures to treat everyday illnesses. Some of these probably worked. But others were based on superstition and 'magic', and probably did not work. Some treatments were based on the theory of the four humours (see Source C on page 82). Look at the following treatments for everyday illnesses.

ILLNESS	TREATMENT	
Toothache	Burn a candle close to the tooth. Hold a basin of cold water underneath it to catch the worms escaping the heat.	Toothache
Heart disease	Give the patient a medicine of parsley or sage, powdered animal skull, the juice of a boiled toad and dead insects.	Heart disease
Bad digestion	Remove the bad blood by cutting a vein or by using leeches.	
Eye infection	Make an eye-ointment from onion, garlic and wine. Strain through a cloth. Rub on the infection with a feather.	Eye infection
Backache	Give the patient two pinches of betony (a herb) and two bowlfuls of sweet wine in hot water. The patient must fast.	
Asthma	Put the lung of a fox into sweetened wine. Drink the mixture.	Backache
Sore eyelid	Poke the sore with nine grains of barley and say: 'Flee, flee, barley chase you.'	

Development of knowledge and skills

Knowledge of the human body

By the end of the Middle Ages, the skills of some doctors were improving. Training now took place in medical schools. In the fourteenth century, Guy De Chauliac, a French doctor, was **dissecting** dead bodies and finding out about the internal organs, muscles, skin, veins and **sinews**.

💡 Why do you think dissecting bodies was useful?

SOURCE F

A dissection at medieval medical school.

Use of painkillers

By the late Middle Ages, more and more doctors were using simple **anaesthetics**. One recipe included the things listed in Source G (see page 86). Some of these anaesthetics actually worked, and sent patients to sleep. But doctors still needed more knowledge about how to get the right mixtures and doses.

Take the **gall** of a boar, **hemlock** juice, lettuce, poppy juice, **henbane**, vinegar and wine. Let him being operated on sit against a good fire and make him drink until he falls asleep. Then you may safely carve him.

A medieval recipe for anaesthetics.

Key words

Gall Digestive juices.
Hemlock and **henbane** Poisonous herbs used in medicine.

The skills of surgeons

When armies went to war in the Middle Ages, they took surgeons with them. There were many wounded people on the battlefield. These surgeons tried out new treatments.

John of Arderne became one of the most famous surgeons in England after working for the army. He did operations, and some of his methods are still used today.

Theoderic of Lucca was a thirteenth-century surgeon who healed wounds with wine. New instruments and tools were also made. But most ordinary people still went to barber-surgeons. They did not trust these 'new' methods.

Plenary

Prepare to feedback some or all of your presentation to the class. **WS**

DID PEOPLE IN THE MIDDLE AGES CARE FOR THEIR CHILDREN?

Objectives

By the end of this section you will be able to answer these questions.
- What were the problems of childbirth in the Middle Ages?
- How were children raised in the Middle Ages?

You will be able to:
- weigh up the evidence
- decide if medieval people cared for their children or not.

Starter

Look at this picture. It shows the birth of a baby in the Middle Ages. What are the chances of the birth being successful?

In pairs, list and explain all the things that would harm this woman's chances of successfully giving birth.

Now turn to another pair and compare your work. Make a complete set of your answers.

List in your books all the things we do today to try to help pregnant women give birth to healthy babies.

Childbirth in the Middle Ages

In the Middle Ages, childbirth was very different to today. Mothers would give birth to as many children as possible, because some would not survive. One out of five pregnant women died either during childbirth or soon after. Over half of all babies born died before they reached their first birthday. This was because of the following things.

- There were no clinics in the Middle Ages, and no scanners and computers. Nobody knew if the baby had any diseases.

- There was no advice about what the pregnant mother should eat, drink or do. Many women worked hard up to the moment the child was born.

- Most women had their babies at home without painkillers. **Midwives** were usually local women with no medical training.

- Operations to deliver babies that might not survive were done by midwives, on kitchen tables and beds. They had unclean hands and wore their normal clothes.

- There were no incubators to keep **premature** babies alive.

How were children brought up in the Middle Ages?

Key words

Midwives Women who help other women deliver their babies.

Premature Born early.

Most ordinary women had to sweep out the houses, cook, brew ale, and look after the animals, the garden and the fruit trees on top of looking after their children.

Women wrapped their children from head to toe in bandages, so they could not move. This was called swaddling. Some mothers hung their babies on hooks to keep them out of harm's way.

How did children die?

Coroners held investigations called inquests about the death of children (see pages 90-1).

A medieval woman nursing her baby while cooking at the same time.

- Half of the deaths of children less than a year old happened while they had been left alone and had fallen into fires.
- Older children sometimes died as they tried to copy their mother or father.
  - A two year-old girl tried to stir a pot of hot water. But she tipped it over herself and was scalded to death.
  - A three year-old boy was watching his father cut wood when the blade of the axe flew off the handle and struck him.

TASKS...

1 Do you think the deaths of the children described above could have been avoided? How? Write down your ideas.

How did people react to the death of a child?

The stories about children's deaths might make you think they were unloved. But this is not necessarily true. Families could be punished if their babies died by falling into fires. Priests often warned parents not to leave their babies alone. Laws said that, when the death of an infant was suspicious, the parents would be questioned. This would show whether or not the parents had looked after the child properly.

The figure of Death (the skeleton) taking a young child from a poor house.

💡 Do you think parents were responsible for the accidental deaths of their children in the Middle Ages?

Coroners

People did take the death of a child seriously. Any mysterious death had to be investigated by a coroner. He would get statements from the family and neighbours about how the child had died. This would include details like:

- what the child was doing before he or she died
- the names of witnesses
- the time and date
- the age of the child.

The coroner then had to inspect the child's body by stripping it and looking at the wounds. He would try to find the cause of death. He also had to collect the taxes that were used to pay for prayers for the dead child. Other witnesses had to say whether the family was honest.

Did parents love their children?

Many stories describe the sadness of families whose children died in accidents. Look at the example below.

SOURCE C

A girl of three years old was sitting under some firewood with her friends. A huge trunk fell down. It threw her on her back in the mud, pinning her down, so that she died. Her friends all ran away. The child's father came to see what had happened. His heart was filled with sadness. Lifting the log with some difficulty, he raised her in his hands. Then groaning and wailing, he made for the church.

From a collection of fifteenth-century stories.

💡 If families were so upset by the deaths of their children, why didn't they do more to protect them?

People in the Middle Ages did not shower their children with love. Life was very difficult, and parents wanted to help their children to survive. The parents had to make sure their children learned how to look after themselves.

TASKS...

1 Use the information you have read to decide whether medieval people cared for their children or not. Study the information and read the following statement:
'Medieval parents were cruel. They did not properly care for, or look after, their children.'

(a) Do you agree or disagree with this statement?

(b) Draw a chart like the one below. Fill it in by using evidence from pages 87–91.

Parents did care for their children	Parents did not care for their children

(c) What is your overall conclusion? Share your ideas with a partner and listen to what he or she has to say.

EXTENSION TASK...

2 Look again at the information about the death of a child in Source C on page 91. Imagine you are the coroner who has to write a report about why the child died. Look again at all the information about how coroners carried out their work on pages 90–1. Use the guide below to help you with your report. **WS**

- Start the report by saying how the child died.

- Include a paragraph on the evidence of the child's family.
  - How did they discover the child?
  - What were they doing at the time the child was killed?

- Include a paragraph that gives details of the child.
  - What was her name?
  - How old was she?
  - How did she die?
  - What were her injuries?

- Include a paragraph on other witnesses.
  - Who were they?
  - Did they see the accident?
  - Did they know the family?
  - Is the family good and caring?

- Finish the report by saying if you think someone should be charged with murder.

Plenary

From all the work you have done in this section, pick out one thing that best shows whether:

- parents did care for their children
- parents did not care for their children.

Explain why you have chosen each piece of evidence.

HOW HEALTHY AND HYGIENIC WERE TOWNS IN THE MIDDLE AGES?

Objectives

By the end of this section you will be able to answer these questions.

• What was the state of health in a medieval town?

• Who was to blame for the state of the town?

You will also take part in an investigation about the state of a medieval town.

Starter

SOURCE A

Now wash your hands

SOURCE B

Westminster Litter Law
£10 Fixed Penalty
Put litter in the bin

SOURCE C

MAXIMUM PENALTY
£1000

CLEAN IT UP!

*Sources A, B and C are signs that we encounter in modern life. They are examples of signs about **hygiene**.*

💡 In pairs, discuss the meaning of each sign. Are words or pictures being used, or both? Will the message of the sign be clear to someone who does not understand English?

💡 What would happen if you did not do what the sign said?

Key words

Hygiene This is about making sure that living conditions are clean so that people stay healthy.

Investigating Cessville – a medieval town

Study the picture of an imaginary medieval town, called Cessville, below.

💡 What do you learn about living conditions from the picture?

💡 What do you think it would have been like to live there?

TASKS...

You are going to investigate the state of health and hygiene in Cessville – an imaginary medieval town. Your task is to decide who is to blame for the poor living conditions.

1 Read the information about the people who live in Cessville on pages 96–7.
  (a) For each person, list all the activities that you think are unhygienic.
  (b) How might these activities affect the people of Cessville?

Who was to blame for the state of Cessville?

All of the following people live in the imaginary medieval town of Cessville.

Mr Brown and Mr Green of Thomas Row *live in one of the poorest parts of Cessville. The houses are packed together and there are no proper drains. They use a bucket for a toilet. Mr Brown tips his sewage into the river. Mr Green piles his up outside his house and hopes it will be washed away by the rain. Everyone else in the street does the same.*

Mr Bullstrode *is a builder and makes a lot of money from building houses. He has been told that all new houses must be built with a cesspit (where you get rid of sewage). These are quite expensive to make. He does not want to talk about the incident last year, when a man fell through a rotten floor and drowned in the cesspit of a house that he had built.*

Mrs Atkins *is a water seller who likes to get fresh water from a local spring. She gets a good price for it from rich people. Most ordinary people get their water from polluted rivers. Sometimes, Mrs Atkins tells her poorer customers that she is selling them fresh water, but she is really selling them water that comes directly from the dirty river.*

Mrs Walters and her daughter, Mary, *live on Cheapside. Mrs Walters tries to keep her children dressed in clean clothes. Her daughter Mary helps her with the washing. They soak the clothes in the river, then beat them with a heavy bat to loosen the dirt. They use plant sap to remove the worst stains. To make a lather, they use chopped-up conkers.*

Councillor Clifford *lives in a mansion just outside the town. He does not believe it is the council's job to keep the town clean. He thinks the town is dirty because the people have made it that way. He was against paying people to become 'rakers' to keep the streets clean. However, he does agree that people who drop rubbish in the streets should be arrested.*

Mr Bates is a butcher, and he has his own shop. He only sells the best quality meat. He is ashamed to admit that he was arrested last year for throwing rotten blood and meat into the street. He says he had nowhere else to put it. He is worried about the state of Cessville. He thinks drains should be laid everywhere, and not just in the richer areas.

Richard Cobb and Elizabeth Burns are rakers. They work in a team with a horse, a cart and rakes. Each team is given an area of the town to keep clean. Richard and Elizabeth never seem to have enough time to take the rubbish away. They have been in court, accused of moving rubbish from their own streets and dumping it into other streets.

Thomas Scott is homeless and sleeps rough. He has bad habits and a short temper. Last year he was fined by the court after he beat up two men. They had complained that they had seen him urinating in the street instead of using the privy (toilet).

Silas Smythe owns a large amount of the land around Cessville. He often makes the journey into town to collect the piles of waste that lie outside houses. He pays good money to use it for manure on his fields to help his crops to grow. He would be against any attempts to stop people from piling up their sewage outside their houses.

Plenary

Clearly more than one person is to blame for the state of Cessville. Place the characters in order. Put who you think is most to blame at the top and who is least to blame at the bottom. Be ready to explain your choices.

WAS MEDIEVAL MEDICINE ALL 'DOOM AND GLOOM'?

Objectives

By the end of this section you will be able to answer this question.

• What were the good and bad things about medicine and health during the Middle Ages?

You will also produce a piece of writing about whether the state of medicine and health was better in 1500 than it was in 1066.

Starter

Look at Source A. Use the 5Ws (who, when, where, what and why?) to find out as much as you can from this picture. Share your questions with the class.

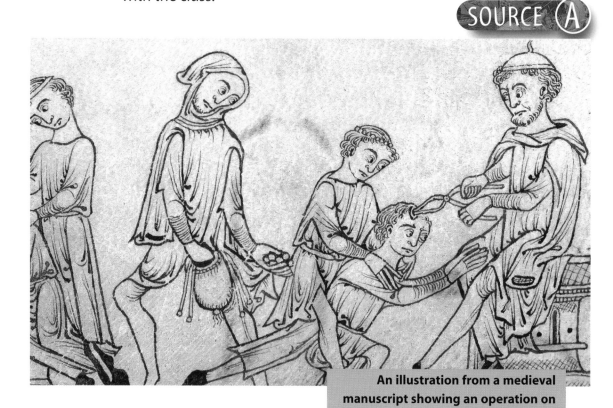

An illustration from a medieval manuscript showing an operation on a patient's head.

How would you feel about medieval doctors and medicine if you had been operated on in this way?

Two views about medicine in the Middle Ages

Doctors are trained in universities, but they still use old treatments. The new medical schools do not affect barber-surgeons, who carry on using the same methods as before. People generally have better houses and eat better food these days. Even so, they don't tend to live to old age. No one knows exactly what causes disease. Deadly infections kill thousands.

Since the 1300s, there have been universities where doctors were trained. Armies take doctors to war with them, where they get experience as surgeons. Laws are passed to clean up towns. New ideas are reaching Europe from Arab doctors. People are beginning to think for themselves. Gradually people are challenging old beliefs. New ideas are on the way!

TASKS...

1 (a) Summarise the viewpoint of each speaker on page 99.

(b) Which of the two views on page 99 gives the best description of medical development during the Middle Ages?

2 (a) Look back over this chapter. In pairs, think about the development of medicine. You should make notes on:

- childbirth
- raising children
- ideas about the causes of disease
- surgeons and operations
- health and hygiene in towns.

(b) What is your view of the question:
'Was medieval medicine all doom and gloom?'

Discuss this in pairs, then join another pair and continue your discussion.

EXTENSION TASK...

3 Produce a piece of writing to answer the following question:
'Was medieval medicine all doom and gloom?'
Use the following guide to help you write your essay. **ws**

- Write an introduction.

- Put each new point in a separate paragraph.

- Support the argument in each paragraph by adding evidence from your reading.

- Use connectives. For example:
  - when comparing and contrasting, use equally, similarly, likewise, whereas, instead of
  - when supporting your views with evidence, use for example, such as, for instance, as shown by.

- Write a summary and conclusion that sets out your overall opinion.

Plenary

You have learned a lot of new words in this chapter. You could play a word game like 'Word bingo' or 'Odd One Out' to test how much you have learned. **ws**

4

WHAT WERE PEOPLE'S BELIEFS IN THE MIDDLE AGES?

TIMELINE
RELIGION IN THE MIDDLE AGES
– some important dates

1066 The Normans invade and change the Church

1100 The Normans start building lots of new churches and cathedrals

1170 Thomas Becket, Archbishop of Canterbury, is killed in Canterbury Cathedral

1205 King John argues with the Pope – the person in charge of the Catholic Church

This chapter looks at people's beliefs in the Middle Ages.

- It looks first at the main beliefs people had at the time.

- Then it describes life in a monastery, what pilgrimages were and why people went on Crusades.

- Finally, it considers the supernatural.

There are some tasks and activities at the end of this chapter.

💡 *What do we believe in today? In groups, list three things you believe in. When you have finished, compare your list to the group next to you. What do they believe in?*

WHAT DID PEOPLE BELIEVE ABOUT RELIGION?

Objectives

By the end of this section you will be able to answer this question.
• What were the main beliefs of medieval people?
You will also use sources to gather evidence of what people believed in.

Starter

Discuss the things that you think medieval people would have believed in. Write a list and keep this for later!

How sources help us to understand what medieval people believed in

In the Middle Ages most people in England believed in God. England was a Christian country and English people were members of the Roman Catholic Church. Religion at this time was very important. A small number of people in England were Jews.

If you could travel back to the Middle Ages and interview someone about his or her beliefs, the person might say:

I believe that if I commit lots of sins I will go to hell.

I believe that I must live my life according to the Ten Commandments in the Bible.

I believe that I must pray to the saints and go on religious trips.

I believe that I must trust the local priest.

We know that this is what people believed in because of the evidence they left. Look closely at Sources A to D, which show pictures from the time.

A wall picture from a medieval church.

Illustration from a fourteenth-century English manuscript. It shows an angel and a devil.

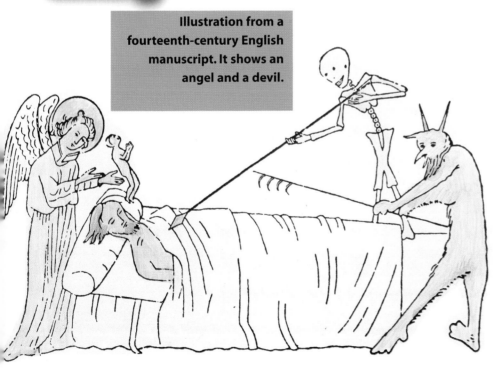

A fifteenth-century picture showing someone being punished.

TASKS...

1 In pairs, use the 5Ws strategy to find out as much as you can about Sources A to D – *who, when, where, what* and *why*?

SOURCE D

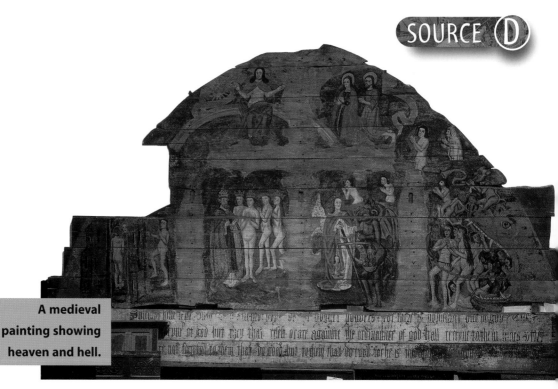

A medieval painting showing heaven and hell.

TASKS...

2 What do Sources A to D tell us about what people believed in the Middle Ages? Here are some words you could use to help you with your answers.

hell	devil	angels	heaven	sinners

You could also make a chart like the one below. This will help you to summarise your answers. An example has been done for you. **WS**

	What the picture actually shows	What the picture tells us about people's beliefs in the Middle Ages
Source A	People being boiled alive or roasted over flames.	People must have believed that hell was a terrible place to go.
Source B		
Source C		
Source D		

3 Look at your chart. Now summarise all you know about what people believed in the Middle Ages. **WS**

Plenary

Look back at the list you made at the beginning of this section. Do you still agree with this list? Explain why or why not.

WHO KILLED NOVICE JOHN?

By the end of this section you will find out:
- What was it like to be a monk or a nun?
- How important was religion in the Middle Ages?

You will also:
- understand that being an historian is a bit like being a detective
- analyse evidence to solve a murder investigation.

Starter

What do you think a monk or nun looks like? Have you ever seen one? What was the person wearing?

In pairs, discuss your answers. You could draw pictures to describe your answers.

Monasteries, convents and the people who lived in them

In the Middle Ages, some people such as monks and nuns lived in religious communities called monasteries or convents. The rules in these communities were strict and the clothes worn by the monks or nuns were simple.

- The monks would shave the tops of their heads, so that they had a bald circle shape.
- A nun would wear a wimple, a hat that hid much of her face.

People who joined religious communities promised to give up everything they owned. They also made a promise of chastity, which meant they would not have sexual relationships. Finally, they promised the abbot or abbess (the head of the monasteries and convents) that they would devote their lives to God.

SOURCE (A)

Nuns at prayer.

Life was hard for the monks and nuns. They spent a lot of time praying. They often had little to do with the outside world. When they weren't praying, they worked long hours in the fields, or cared for sick or dying people.

Some monks illustrated, or illuminated, manuscripts, which was the way books were produced at this time. Look at Sources B, C and D, which show illustrated manuscripts.

💡 Why do you think people became monks and nuns?

SOURCE (B)

An illuminated manuscript.

SOURCE (C)

An illustrated manuscript.

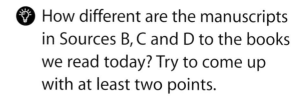

SOURCE D

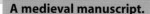

A medieval manuscript.

💡 How different are the manuscripts in Sources B, C and D to the books we read today? Try to come up with at least two points.

Bad behaviour!

Not all monks and nuns behaved well! Some monks and nuns often broke their religious vows during the Middle Ages. Reports from the time tell of cases of drinking and gambling, as well as laziness, greed and fighting. Some nuns even had children!

But most monks and nuns followed the rules of their religion. They lived a life of prayer and discipline and did not get into bad habits.

A murder investigation

If there was a murder in a religious community, the Church would investigate what happened. Imagine you have been asked by the abbott of Hestoneded Abbey to solve a crime. One of the abbey's new monks, called Novice John, has been killed. You must find the murderer. This investigation will involve a number of stages, and the information on pages 109–112 will help you.

Who murdered the novice monk?

TASKS...

You are about to solve a murder. Here's how …

Stage 1: gathering evidence

Ask the abbot for information to help you solve the crime.

You need to know:

- the times of all the religious services
- how many monks there are in the abbey
- who does which job.

The abbott gives you two pieces of evidence – **Evidence A** and **Evidence B**. Read these carefully.

Key words

Matins Morning prayer.
Lauds A short church service.
Prime A service held at dawn.
Terce A service followed by meditation.
Sext A service after which monks had a wash.
Vespers A service held in the early evening.
Compline The last service of the day.

Evidence A:
the times of services and meals in the monastery

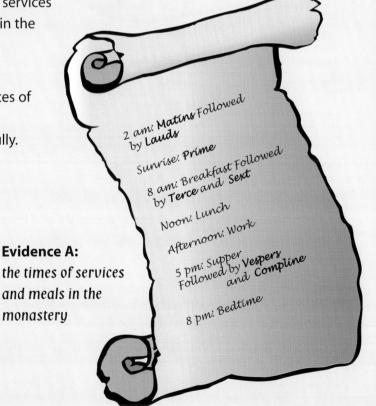

2 am: **Matins** Followed by **Lauds**

Sunrise: **Prime**

8 am: Breakfast Followed by **Terce** and **Sext**

Noon: Lunch

Afternoon: Work

5 pm: Supper Followed by **Vespers** and **Compline**

8 pm: Bedtime

Evidence B: *the monks and their jobs*

Abbott — Person in charge of the monastery

Prior — The deputy abbot

Almoner — Person in charge of giving alms (money) to the poor

Cellarer — Person who looks after the food and drink

Chamberlain — Person who looks after monks' clothing and living area

Infirmarian — Person who looks after the infirmary, where the sick are tended

Novices — Young men who have joined as trainee monks

Kitchener — The cook, who works closely with the cellarer

Precentor — Person who looks after Church services

Stage 2: reading statements

Now read the monks' statements on pages 111–112. For each one fill in an evidence chart like the one below.

This chart should contain the following information.

- Who gave the statement?
- What is his job?
- Is there anything suspicious about him?
- Why might he have killed Novice John?

An example has been done for you, so you can see what type of thing you should be writing on this sheet. **WS**

Name	Reasons for suspicion
Precentor	Looks after the Church services.
	Was the last one to see John alive.
	Had a candle, and there was wax found next to the body.
	There doesn't seem to be a motive.

Stage 3: deciding who committed the murder

After you have read through all the statements and filled in your evidence charts, think about who you suspect of murdering Novice John. In your groups, can you agree on your suspect?

Stage 4: catching the suspect

Now that you have agreed who murdered Novice John, design a 'Wanted' poster that may help to catch him. Your poster should have:

- a big, bold heading – something like: 'WANTED FOR THE MURDER OF NOVICE JOHN'
- the name of the suspect
- the reasons you suspect this person of murder.

The precentor's statement

I was the last person to see Novice John alive. He was very unhappy. I know that his mother came to see him recently. She is such a kind woman. Nobody knows who Novice John's father was.

I left John to lock up because he said that he wanted to stay behind and pray. So I took my candle and left. Then I heard he was dead. The abbot called me straight away.

The abbot's statement

I found the body after Compline. At first, I didn't see the body because my candle was so low. It was lying at the base of the stairs.

John worked with the precentor. We haven't moved a thing at the scene of the murder. As you will see, there is a large pool of wax by his body. There are also muddy footprints leading from the body up the stairs. It looks like Novice John was stabbed with a short knife, possibly the kind used to sharpen quills (feathers used to write with).

I don't know who would murder Novice John. He was so young and didn't have any enemies. He was so happy here.

The monks have little contact with outsiders – apart from the poor who come to the abbey to receive money. The monks need permission from me if they want to have guests or travel. I am the only one who is allowed to leave the abbey without telling anyone.

The chamberlain's statement

My job is to look after the monks' clothes and the dormitories. I saw Novice John yesterday and he was very serious. Usually he would smile a lot, and would try to tell me plenty of news using sign language, as speaking is forbidden. He was such a nice young man and he had only been here a year.

John had a visit from his mother a few weeks ago and ever since then he has been quiet. Lately, I have been teaching him how to illustrate manuscripts. He has learned how to sharpen quills.

The cellarer's statement

I am in charge of food and drink. I had a busy day as always. After Prime, I had to check the ale and pour some for breakfast. I also had to make sure we had enough bread.

The lunch was easy – the monks had ham. In the afternoon, I caught some trout in our fish-pond and cooked it in time for supper. I went out after Vespers to feed the pigs and took a stroll down to the river to visit the toilet. It's very muddy down there at the moment. The river was flooded for weeks.

Vespers was the last time I saw Novice John. I feel sorry for the Abbot. He looks so worried. A murder is the last thing he needs. In fact, he has looked worried for weeks.

The almoner's statement

I was giving out money to the poor all afternoon. It was quite busy today, but it has been all year. It is always busy when there has been a bad harvest. There has been little work with so much land under water after the floods. Then there were the usual poor from the village, including Novice John's mother. She always takes her money without saying a word.

After the poor had left or were in their rooms for the night, I cleaned the floors of the alms room, which were covered with mud. Then I spent an hour in the study in which we illustrate manuscripts. After supper, I collected a candle and went to Vespers. I stayed on in silent prayer until Compline, then went to my room.

The kitchener's statement

Everyone liked Novice John. I can't imagine who would try to kill him. They said he was stabbed. I counted my knives, but they were all here.

I feel so sorry for the Abbot. He has worked very hard to make this monastery successful. I saw him yesterday down by the river cutting reeds, which we will use for basket making. He must have worked several hours that day, because it was getting dark by the time he came back from the river. He wasn't in Vespers, but he often missed chapel in the evening.

Plenary

Look back at pages 106–112. In pairs, discuss what you have learned about the lives of monks and nuns. Then discuss how important you think the Church and religion were in the Middle Ages. Write out three questions you would like to ask about religion in the Middle Ages.

WHAT AND WHO WERE PILGRIMS?

Objectives

By the end of this section you will be able to answer these questions.
- Who went on pilgrimages?
- How did they travel?
- Why was Canterbury such a special place?
- Why did Henry II quarrel with Thomas Becket?

You will organise information and present your results.

Starter

Many people in the Middle Ages went on a pilgrimage, which is a journey to visit a religious place. The people who go on a pilgrimage are known as pilgrims. With a partner, look at Source A.

Pilgrims on the road to Canterbury.

⚘ What types of people can you see in Source A? Try to write down five words to describe the scene.

⚘ Can you think of any places of pilgrimage today?

Sites of pilgrimage

It could take pilgrims a long time to reach their destinations. The most popular place of pilgrimage in England was at Canterbury Cathedral, where St Thomas Becket was buried (see pages 117–119).

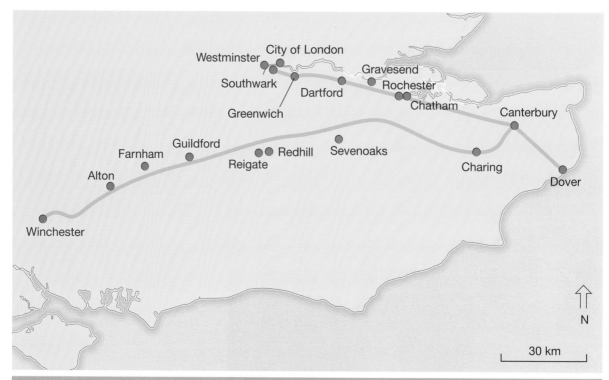

Routes to Canterbury from London, Kent and the south coast of England.

But people didn't only go on pilgrimages in Europe. Some travelled to Jerusalem in the Holy Land to visit the sites connected to Jesus' life.

Why do you think people went on pilgrimages?

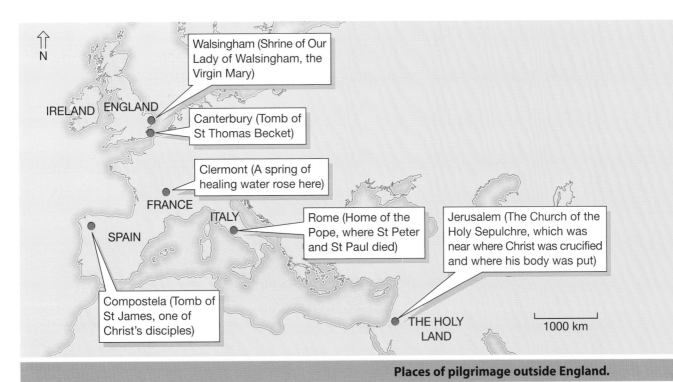

Places of pilgrimage outside England.

TASKS...

1 In pairs, you are going to investigate why people went on pilgrimages. You will either produce a booklet or give a presentation to the class.

Your investigation should be based around questions like these:

- What kind of people went on pilgrimages?
- What were their jobs?
- Why did people go on pilgrimages?

2 To help you gather information, you could put your ideas on a mind map. Use the outline below to help you get started. **WS**

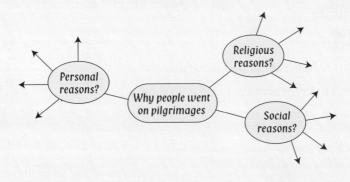

Medieval pilgrims

So, why did people go on pilgrimage? As you read about each
of the characters you will notice the name St Thomas.
Remember what these characters say about him.

Knight

I am a knight. I have fought all over the world. I am a noble
man. I am going on the pilgrimage to thank God for safe
return from war.

I am a squire. This means I am learning how to be a knight. I
have already fought in wars in France. I am on the pilgrimage
with my father.

Squire

Wife of Bath

I am a cloth-maker from Bath. I enjoy pilgrimages. In fact, I have been to
Jerusalem twice, Rome, Compostella and Cologne. I think that going on
pilgrimages to places abroad helps me get closer to God.

I am a monk. I enjoy the food and company on this trip.
At supper last night, I ate a whole roast swan! I want to
visit the holy shrines but I also like pilgrimages because
they are good fun.

Monk

Friar

I am a Friar called Hubert. I make money from begging.
Pilgrimages are like nice holidays!

I am a nun and try to live close to God by setting an
example to others. I want to visit the tomb of St Thomas
to pray there.

Nun

Miller

There are lots of us young millers on
pilgrimage. I like cracking jokes and having
fun. St Thomas – why is he important?

The struggle between the Church and the king

The Church was very important to people in the Middle Ages. Most people believed that God controlled everything. The church was central to village life and everyone would go there every Sunday. The Pope was the head of the Church, not the king. However, many kings tried to control the Church.

Thomas Becket was a close friend of Henry II. Henry made Becket Archbishop of Canterbury in 1162. As archbishop, Becket would have to listen to the Pope not Henry. This led to a bitter quarrel between Henry and Becket, because Henry was angry that Becket now took the side of the Pope instead of the king.

The death of Thomas Becket

A picture of 1190 showing Thomas Becket's death.

The murder of Thomas Becket, from a fifteenth-century manuscript.

TASKS...

1. Read statements (a) to (i) which describe a quarrel between King Henry II and Thomas Becket. These statements give clues about why Becket was killed. The only problem is, the statements are not in the right order. With a partner, work out the right chronological (time) order of the statements. **WS**

(a) The Church was rich and had great power.

(b) As part of his attempt to control the Church, Henry II made his friend Thomas Becket Archbishop of Canterbury in 1162.

(c) Becket returned to England in 1170, but still refused to do what Henry told him.

(d) In 1164 Becket was forced to go into hiding in France.

(e) Four of Henry's knights rode to Canterbury. They burst into the cathedral and killed Becket.

(f) Pope Alexander III was upset by Becket's murder. In 1173, Becket was made a saint and 29 December was made St Thomas' Day.

(g) Henry's temper snapped. He cried: 'Will no one rid me of this difficult priest?'

(h) Pilgrims began to visit the shrine of Becket. In 1174, Henry II visited the cathedral. He was beaten by the monks as punishment for the murder of Becket.

(i) Henry's appointment of Becket as archbishop went wrong. In 1163, he refused to hand priests over to Henry's courts for trial.

TASKS...

2 Look at Sources B and C on page 117, which will give more evidence about Becket. Think about which person in each source is Becket. List the clues that tell you what happened to Becket.

The importance of Becket's tomb

People were angry about Becket's death and soon began flocking to his tomb. They believed that the place where Becket had been killed was a holy place.

TASKS...

1 Why do you think Becket's tomb at Canterbury was such an important shrine? In pairs, come up with as many reasons as you can.

2 Write a catchy newspaper headline telling of Becket's murder.

Plenary

Write a one minute newsflash on the death of Thomas Becket, to present to the class. **WS**

WHY GO ON A CRUSADE?

By the end of this section you will be able to answer these questions.
- What are the three most popular religions in the world?
- What were the Christian attitudes towards the Crusades?
- What were the Muslim attitudes towards the Crusades?

You will see that there are usually at least two sides to every argument.

Starter

Whose point of view is right?

It is normal for people to have very strong opinions, or beliefs. But, not everybody agrees on what is right and wrong. Here are some things that people often feel differently about:

- *the death penalty*
- *eating meat.*

💡 *What strong opinions, or beliefs, do you have?*

When people have strong opinions about things, it is often very hard to agree. In this section you will discover how people with very different religious beliefs behaved towards each other during the Middle Ages.

💡 *Can you think of an example where groups of people are in conflict because of their different views? Brainstorm and make a list.*

The world's three most popular religions

Jerusalem is a very important city for three of the world's most popular religions.

Key words

Muslim Someone who believes in the teachings of the Prophet Muhammad. His or her holy book is the Koran.

Christian Someone who believes that Jesus Christ is the Son of God. His or her holy book is the Bible.

Jew Someone who believes in one God. His or her holy book is the Tenakh.

Islam

Jerusalem is home to the Dome of the Rock. In AD 620, the founder of Islam, the Prophet Muhammad, arrived in Jerusalem. The mosque that was built on the Dome is very important to **Muslims**.

Christianity

The hill of Calvary in Jerusalem was the place where Jesus Christ died. Jesus also preached on the Mount of Olives in the city. From the fourth century, **Christian** pilgrims from all over the world came to visit Jerusalem.

Judaism

In AD 70, the Romans destroyed the most important temple of the Jewish faith that had been built by King David. But Jerusalem is still one of the holiest cities for Jews.

Church of St Mary Magdalen

Mount of Olives

St Stephen's Gate

Church of St Anne

Church of the Holy Sepulchre

Dome of the Rock

N

Monastery

Pool of the Patriarch

Church of St James

David's Gate

St Thomas

David's Tower

St James

Church of the Virgin

Tanners' Gate

Cemetery

Zion Gate

Germanus' Pool

Mount Zion

Pool of Siloam

0.5 km

Sites of religious importance to:

Christians

Jews

Muslims

Areas of Jerusalem important to Christians, Jews and Muslims.

Arguments about Jerusalem and the Holy Land

The city of Jerusalem and the area around it is known as the Holy Land. This area has been argued over for years by Christians and Muslims. Your aim is to find out about the different attitudes most Christians and Muslims had towards each other between the eleventh and thirteenth centuries.

The Muslims and the Christians

Until the eleventh century, all pilgrims were able to visit Jerusalem. The city was controlled by Muslims. In the 1070s, Jerusalem fell under the control of the Seljuk Turks, who were also Muslim. However, the Seljuk Turks were less willing to let Christian pilgrims visit Jerusalem.

As a result, at Clermont in 1095, Pope Urban II appealed to Christians all over the world for help in fighting in a Crusade against Muslims.

Crusaders came from all over Europe in answer to the Pope's appeal. The most famous English person who fought in the Crusades was King Richard I (Richard the Lionheart).

💡 Have you heard the word Crusade before?

💡 What do you think people were fighting for?

Pope Urban II's attitudes

The Pope was the most important person in the Christian world, and his views were very important. Sources A and C are by Pope Urban II. Source B shows Christian attitudes towards the Muslims.

TASKS...

1 In pairs, look at Sources A, B and C. Pick at least three words or phrases from these sources that tell us about Christian attitudes towards Muslims. You can put these words on a chart like the one below. **WS**

	Keywords and phrases to describe source
Source A	
Source B	
Source C	

SOURCE A

A horrible race has attacked Jerusalem. They have destroyed the churches of God. Jerusalem is now the prisoner of the enemies of Jesus Christ. These people don't even know how to pray to God.

Pope Urban II speaking in 1095.

SOURCE B

A thirteenth-century illustration showing Christian attitudes towards Muslims.

SOURCE C

I know that many of you have heard about the wild attacks of the Muslims against Christian churches. They have even taken over the Holy City of Jerusalem.

Pope Urban II writing in 1096.

The Crusades

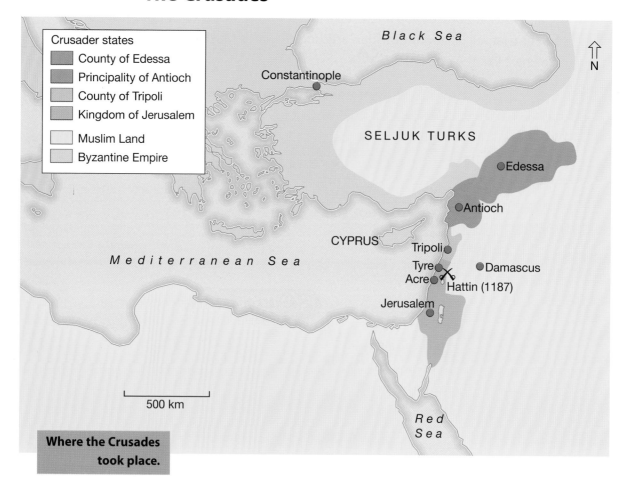

Where the Crusades took place.

Over the next 300 years, Christian armies tried to conquer Jerusalem.

The First Crusade

The First Crusade started in 1096 and lasted three years. Many areas of land came under Christian rule. But, by the end of the First Crusade, only half the number of knights who had set out to fight returned home.

The fight for the city of Jerusalem

The biggest success of the First Crusade was the capture of Jerusalem. The Christian attack on Jerusalem was fierce.

- Christian archers fired arrows.
- Steel hooks attached to long ropes were catapulted onto the city walls, to pull them down.
- Battering rams were used to break down the city gates.
- Boulders were rolled into the moat so that the Crusaders could cross.

The defending Turks resisted the attack on their city.

- They used bales of straw to block the gates.
- They threw pots of burning liquid over the walls onto the Crusaders.
- They dragged the dead bodies of the Crusaders onto the citywalls, so they could steal their weapons and armour.

It took the Crusaders one month to break through the city walls. Once inside, they burned buildings, they stole precious goods, and murdered 70,000 Turks and Jews. The Crusaders now claimed Jerusalem as a Christian city.

💡 What do you think the people of Jerusalem would have thought of their new Christian rulers?

The struggles between Muslims and Christians continue …
Between 1096 and 1291 there were six different Crusades. They were violent and caused the hatred between Muslims and Christians to deepen. But sometimes Muslims and Christians tolerated each other and even became friends.

The Crusades continue …

1145–9 The Second Crusade. The Crusaders actually lose land!

1187 Saladin, a Muslim leader, defeats the Christian armies and conquers Jerusalem.

1189–92 The Third Crusade. This was led by Richard of England and King Phillip of France.

1202–4 The Fourth Crusade. Some people say the Crusaders are selfish because the crusade is more about winning trade routes than religious belief.

1217–22 The Fifth Crusade.

1228–9 The Sixth Crusade. The Christians retake Jerusalem.

1244 The Crusaders are thrown out of Jerusalem by the Muslim leader as-Salil Ismail.

1291 The Crusaders leave the Holy Land.

The Children's Crusade

It was not just adults who went on Crusades. In 1212, hundreds of French and German children decided they would go to the Holy Land and recapture Jerusalem from the Muslims.

The German children reached Pisa (in Italy), and the French got to the port of Marseilles. They hoped for ships to take them to the Holy Land. The German children set sail, but were never heard of again. The French children were tricked by two Christian merchants and were sold as slaves to Muslim nobles and merchants.

TASKS...

1 Work in pairs. One of you will take the role of a Christian child. The other will take the role of a Muslim child. Take it in turns to explain to each other your different attitudes towards the Crusades.

You should try to argue for your religion. Try to convince the other person of your opinion.

SOURCE D

A Christian came to us asking to see Saladin. She said that her daughter had been taken in the night by Muslims. Saladin sent a horseman to look for the girl. They both returned not long after. The girl's mother cried with joy.

Adapted from Baha ad-Din Ibn Shaddad, writing at the time about Saladin.

Different views

Look again at Sources A, B and C on page 123. Then study Sources D to H, which are all written or drawn by Christians and Muslims. **WS**

SOURCE E

As soon as one of our knights climbed the wall of the city, the defenders ran away. Our men chased them, killing as many as they could. Soon our soldiers took the whole city, and seized gold, silver and houses full of treasure. The dead Muslims were piled up high outside the city and their bodies were burned.

Adapted from the Christian story Deeds of the Franks, written by an unknown author. He was in Jerusalem in 1099 when the Crusaders took the city.

SOURCE F

This picture shows one aspect of Muslim culture. Here you can see a garden in Baghdad where rich men are being entertained.

SOURCE G

The land where Christ was born has fallen into the hands of pagans. The bodies of saints have been fed to animals and our churches have been turned into stables. Those of you who fight to free the land of Christ will be given a place in heaven by God.

Pope Celestine III speaking in 1195, encouraging Christians to fight in the Holy Land.

Key words

Pagan A person who does not believe in God but worships the natural world.

WHAT WERE PEOPLE'S BELIEFS IN THE MIDDLE AGES?

127

Jerusalem is where the Prophet Muhammad made his journey to heaven from. We do not want to give it up to the Christian beasts who are only interested in land and riches.

By a Muslim writer in the twelfth century.

TASKS ...

1 In pairs, look at all the sources in this section. Now pick at least three words or phrases from each source that tells us about Muslim attitudes towards the Holy Land and the Crusaders. You can put these words on a chart like the one below.

	Keywords and phrases to describe source
Source A	
Source B	
Source C	
Source D	
Source E	

2 You have now learned about the attitudes of the Muslims and Christians. Discuss in groups why people from these two religions had such different viewpoints. One person in the group should make a note of the ideas you come up with. Each group could then tell its conclusions to the whole class. Here are some questions you could discuss.

💡 Why do the Christians and Muslims have different attitudes towards the Crusades?

💡 Do you think they were sometimes wrong in their views?

💡 What can we learn about the Crusades?

Plenary

Do you think that people with different beliefs can live peacefully together? Give a reason for your answer.

DID PEOPLE IN THE MIDDLE AGES BELIEVE IN THE SUPERNATURAL?

By the end of this section you will be able to answer these questions.
- Did people believe only in God?
- What else did people believe in?

The objective of this section is for you to understand what other things people believed in.

Starter

Why do you think storms happen?
Why does the moon eclipse the sun?
Why do animals catch diseases?
Do UFOs exist?

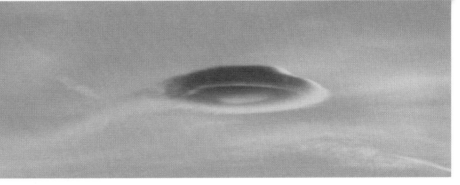

Do UFOs exist? How can we know for certain?

It is possible to find out answers to the first three questions. But we really don't know the answer to the last one.

When people don't know the answer to a question, they sometimes blame the supernatural.

The powers of the Church

In medieval times, things in the natural world that people did not understand were explained as the work of of God. You have already read about the pilgrimages to Canterbury (see pages 114–119). Many pilgrims hoped that they would be cured of illness. The Church explained the supernatural in a number of ways:

* the work of saints
* the work of priests
* superstitions and charms.

The power of Saints

Stories of saints were very popular during the Middle Ages. People also learned about them through paintings, statues and stained glass windows in church.

People would decide which saint to pray to depending on what they wanted. For example, St Christopher protected travellers and so people prayed to him before going on a long journey. Each saint had a special day in the Church calendar. On this day people would go to feasts and celebrations.

Miracles

People thought saints made miracles happen, like curing people of blindness. In the Middle Ages, people often prayed to saints because they wanted them to bring miracles into their lives.

💡 Who do you think would make a modern saint? Can you think of a public figure who sets a good example to us all?

💡 Who do you think would make a modern saint?

Rituals and relics

Rituals

Rituals were another way in which medieval people got closer to God. Rituals were simple actions, such as kneeling during prayer or wearing special clothes. Rituals could also involve religious plays and fasting.

💡 Some tennis players always bounce the ball a certain number of times before they play a point, to bring them good luck. Do you think this is a 'modern ritual'?

💡 Do you carry out any 'modern rituals' in your life?

Relics

Relics were objects which had belonged to a saint. They might be the saint's clothes, hair, nails, or even their bones! People thought these objects would bring them closer to the saint, and so they would travel many miles to visit a relic. Pilgrims would pray to a relic, but touching a relic was even better!

TASKS...

1 Do some research to find out about a medieval saint, ritual or relic. Write a short report to feedback to the class. When you write your report, remember to:
   - State the facts about what you are talking about. You could use the 5Ws – *who*, *what*, *when*, *where* and *why*?
   - Say what was special about that saint, ritual or relic.

TASKS...

2 You are going to answer the key question, '*What were people's beliefs in the Middle Ages?*'

Divide a double page in your book into four equal squares. In each square, write some information about what people believed in. You will need to identify four key beliefs. You could include the following information for each belief:

- What was the belief about?
- How did people behave because of this belief?
- Why did people have this belief?

Plenary

Did you think any of the beliefs from the Middle Ages were ridiculous? Which ones? Why did you think this? How might you explain this to a person from the Middle Ages?

WHO WAS THE BEST AND WHO WAS THE WORST KING, 1087–1307?

5

TIMELINE 1087 to 1307

1087   William the Conqueror dies. His son, William Rufus, becomes King of England.

1100   William Rufus dies. Henry I is made king.

1120   William and Robert, Henry's sons, drown at sea.

1135   Henry I dies leaving the throne to his daughter, Matilda. It is also claimed by his nephew, Stephen of Blois, who becomes king.

1154   Henry II becomes king.

1162   Henry chooses his friend Thomas Becket as Archbishop of Canterbury.

1170   Becket is murdered in Canterbury Cathedral.

1189   Richard I is made king.

1199   John is crowned king.

1215   King John is forced to sign the Magna Carta.

1216   Henry III becomes king at the age of nine.

1272   Edward I becomes king.

1307   Edward I dies.

The rulers of England in the Middle Ages were very powerful. But what kind of people were they? Most kings considered themselves Norman or French as much as English.

- They spoke French.

- Lots of their land was in France.

Ruling England after 1066 was difficult for William the Conqueror because he had conquered the country. Many people didn't accept him as king.

💡 You have already read about William the Conqueror's reign in Chapter 2. What difficulties did William the Conqueror face as king?

Look at the family tree on page 134 to see who the kings of England were between 1087 and 1307.

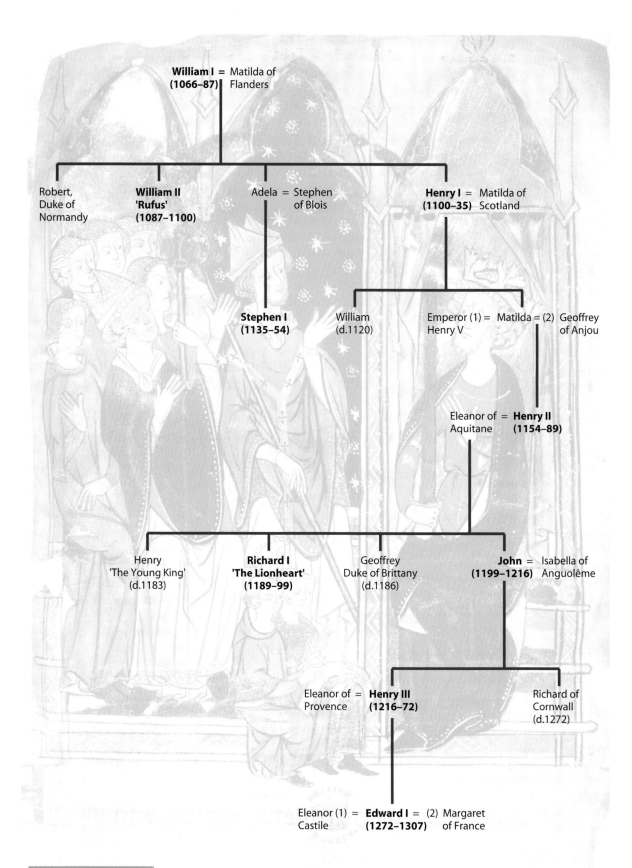

William I = Matilda of
(1066–87) Flanders

Robert, Duke of Normandy

William II 'Rufus' (1087–1100)

Adela = Stephen of Blois

Henry I = Matilda of
(1100–35) Scotland

Stephen I (1135–54)

William (d.1120)

Emperor (1) = Matilda = (2) Geoffrey
Henry V of Anjou

Eleanor of = Henry II
Aquitane (1154–89)

Henry 'The Young King' (d.1183)

Richard I 'The Lionheart' (1189–99)

Geoffrey Duke of Brittany (d.1186)

John = Isabella of
(1199–1216) Anguolême

Eleanor of = Henry III
Provence (1216–72)

Richard of Cornwall (d.1272)

Eleanor (1) = Edward I = (2) Margaret
Castile (1272–1307) of France

Kings of England, 1066 to 1307.

WHAT QUALITIES DOES A KING NEED?

By the end of this section you will be able to answer this question.
• What makes a good king and what makes a bad king?

You will also be investigating:
• The important factors for being a good king.

Starter
Write down three things that you think make a good king. You can make a list or do a spider diagram. Compare your ideas with others in your class.

Important factors for being king
Ruling England in the Middle Ages was a difficult job.

• The most important thing a monarch had to do was keep hold of the throne.

• A good English king was one who could keep the peace. But medieval kings also needed to be good in war.

• They needed to keep their large amount of land in France, deal with Scotland, Wales and Ireland, and end any uprisings at home.

• A good English king also needed to provide good government. Many good kings introduced new ideas to make the country run even more smoothly.

• A son was useful. If everyone knew and agreed who was going to be the next ruler, it would stop people arguing about it.

• So medieval kings needed to have strong personalities. They also needed some luck. Some kings are seen as being good because they were lucky enough to rule in peaceful times.

💡 Jot down the difficulties facing medieval kings. Which do you think would have been the hardest to deal with?

TASKS...

1 **(a)** Get into groups. On a large sheet of paper, copy out the list below. Then discuss whether these things make a good king. Remember that everything on the list is important, but some things are more important than others.

- Dealt well with neighbours.
- Had a male heir who could take over as king.
- Had peaceful relations with the Church.
- Good with the country's money.

- Good at running the country.
- Successful in war.
- Not many rebellions against him.
- Had a strong personality.
- Had few challenges to the throne.

(b) Look back at your own list or spider diagram. Add your own points to the list in Task 1(a).

2 On your own, think about four things on the list that are more important and four things that are less important in making a good king. Then explain your choices to the rest of your group.

3 As a group, draw a chart like the one below. Agree on which four things are more important and which four things are less important, then add them to the chart. **WS**

More important factors	Less important factors

You are now ready to begin working on your answer to the key question: *'Who was the best and who was the worst king, 1087–1307?'*

Plenary

What would make a really bad king? Make a list. Try to think of at least three things.

WILLIAM RUFUS OR HENRY I: WHICH KING WAS BETTER?

Objectives

By the end of this section you will be able to answer this question.
- Who was the better king, William Rufus or Henry I?

By examining the sources, you will be able to:

- compare their reigns
- come to a final decision about who was the better king.

Starter

Look at Sources A and B.

💡 *What does Source A tell us about William Rufus?*

💡 *What does Source B tell us about Henry I?*

William Rufus, who was King of England from 1087 to 1100.

Henry I, who was King of England from 1100 to 1135.

William Rufus

William Rufus got his name because he had red hair, and lots of it! He also had a terrible temper. People were frightened of William, but when they wrote about him, they were very kind.

Peter of Blois, whose words you will read in Source C, didn't like William Rufus. But you might find enough things about William that make you think he was a good king.

William Rufus was William I's second son. When William I died in 1087, his eldest son, Robert, was given Normandy. William Rufus was made king of England. The third son, Henry, was given £5000.

💡 Do you think that William I treated his three sons fairly? Give reasons for your answer.

Henry I

Henry I was born in England. He spoke English as well as French. When William Rufus died in 1100, Robert should have been made king, but he was fighting abroad so Henry made himself king.

TASKS...

1 **(a)** In pairs, read Source C. As you read, pick out three to five words or phrases that show what Peter of Blois thought about William and his followers. Write them down.

(b) Now read Source D. Again, as you read, pick out three to five words or phrases that show what Peter of Blois thought about Henry I. Write them down.

(c) With your partner, decide if Peter of Blois preferred William Rufus or Henry I.

SOURCE C

William Rufus was a strong ruler. He fought hard against any rebellions. Soon there was no one who dared to plot against him.

William did not like the Church and he became an enemy of the Pope. William made his friend, Ranulph, the Bishop of Durham. But Ranulph was a greedy man who helped William get every penny he could from the Church and the people. The worst thing was that William and Ranulph spent the money they stole on having fun.

These were bad times in England. Lots of people were murdered. There was a famine, and an outbreak of disease among men, as well as animals.

Abroad, William got control of Normandy in 1096. He became friendly with the kings of Scotland and Wales.

In the end he was killed in a hunting accident by a man who aimed an arrow at a stag. It missed the stag and pierced the king's chest. The king fell to the earth and died. Not many people were upset at William's death. He died without an heir.

Adapted from Peter of Blois, a Frenchman writing about William Rufus in the thirteenth century.

SOURCE D

Henry, who was cleverer than his two brothers became king after William Rufus. Henry was better suited to being king. Straight away he promised fair rule. He also threw William's friend, Ranulph, into prison.

Henry's brother, Robert, stirred up trouble against him. In 1106 Henry invaded Normandy and defeated his brother's army. He put Robert in prison, where he died.

In 1107 Henry made peace with the Church.

These were good times. England was run very well. Royal courts were fair and honest. The country was doing so well that many people came to England from Normandy. Some monks set up a programme of road building and improving the land.

In 1100 Henry married a Scottish woman, Matilda. She was very popular because she was not French.

Henry and Matilda had four children – two boys and two girls. But tragedy struck. The two sons were drowned in 1120. Henry chose Matilda, his daughter, to be his heir. She was married to a Frenchman called Geoffrey Plantagenet.

By the end of his reign, Henry was quarrelling with Matilda and Geoffrey.

Matilda had a rival who also wanted to claim the throne – her cousin, Stephen of Blois. So the reign of Henry I did not come to a happy end.

Adapted from Peter of Blois, writing in the thirteenth century, on Henry I.

TASKS...

1 Earlier, you made a decision about which king Peter of Blois preferred.
   (a) How did you make this decision?
   (b) Do you think you can trust what Peter of Blois says? Give reasons for your answer.

Plenary

It's now time to make up your own mind about who you think was the better king – William Rufus or Henry I. Copy a spider diagram like the one opposite. Choose who you think is the better king and fill in three things you think are better about this person.

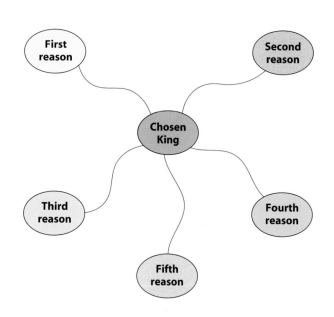

STEPHEN OF BLOIS OR HENRY II: WHICH KING WAS BETTER?

Objectives

By the end of this section you will be able to answer this question.
• Who was the better king: Stephen or Henry II?

By examining the sources, you will be able to spot:
• what is fact and what is opinion.

You will also be able to:
• judge Stephen I and Henry II
• compare the two monarchs and come to a final decision about who was the better king.

Starter

In groups, brainstorm to come up with a list of three monarchs. Are they all kings? Have you included any queens? Do you think only men make good monarchs? Give reasons for your answer.

Stephen of Blois

Stephen of Blois, who was King of England from 1135 to 1154.

William Rufus and Henry I were brothers, but they were very different. On pages 139–40 we read what happened at the end of Henry I's reign. He decided that Matilda (his daughter) would become the next ruler of England.

💡 Do you think people at the time wanted a female monarch?

Stephen of Blois was very unhappy about Matilda becoming queen. His mother, Adela, was Henry I's sister, so he thought he should be king.

Stephen's desire to become king led to a **civil war**. Some barons supported Stephen and other barons supported Matilda. When Henry I died in 1135, Matilda was in France. So Stephen crowned himself king.

The war had a very bad effect on England.

- Barons began to do what they wanted, such as building castles and seizing land.
- The Scots invaded the north of England.
- The Church became more powerful, sometimes more than the king himself.

In 1153, Stephen and Matilda eventually made peace. Matilda would recognise Stephen's right to be king, and Stephen would recognise Matilda's son, Henry, as his successor. A year later, Stephen died and Henry was crowned Henry II.

SOURCE B

Henry II, who was King of England from 1154 to 1189.

Henry II

Henry II was King of England from 1154 to 1189. He married Eleanor of Aquitaine, which gave him plenty of French land, as you can see from the map on page 143.

Henry was clever, but had a terrible temper. He had several sons, but his favourite was John. His sons rebelled against him towards the end of his reign, which made him even angrier.

Henry is often remembered for an argument he had with Thomas Becket. This argument was about priests who had broken the law. Henry wanted Becket to allow them to be tried in his courts, not in Church courts.

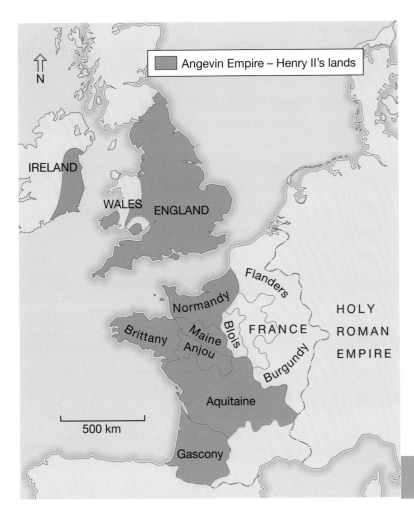

Angevin Empire – Henry II's lands

IRELAND

WALES

ENGLAND

Flanders

Normandy

Brittany

Maine

Blois

Anjou

FRANCE

Burgundy

HOLY
ROMAN
EMPIRE

Aquitaine

500 km

Gascony

Thomas was the Archbishop of Canterbury, the most important churchman in England, so he felt strong enough to refuse. Henry flew into a rage, and four of his knights rode to Canterbury and killed Becket in Canterbury Cathedral.

But it's not fair to remember Henry just as a bad-tempered king. He also made improvements to how the law courts worked and to government taxation.

Henry II's empire during his reign as king.

TASKS...

1 Working in pairs, look at Sources C to F. **WS**

   (a) One of you will read Sources C and D, which are about Stephen. The other should make a list of three questions to ask about Stephen. When you have both finished, try to answer the three questions. Write down the answers.

   (b) Now swap jobs! The person who wrote the questions about Stephen will now read Sources E and F. The person who read Sources C and D will now make a list of three questions to ask about Henry. When you have both finished, try to answer your three questions. Write down the answers.

   (c) Now compare the answers you have for Stephen of Blois with the answers you have for Henry II. Decide which king seems to be the better of the two.

SOURCE C

In the days of Stephen, there was nothing but chaos, war and robbery. The barons of the country rebelled against him. The chaos lasted for the whole time Stephen was king, until the country was in ruins.

A description of Stephen's reign from the twelfth century.

SOURCE D

All of Stephen's reign was overshadowed by war. In 1141, his army was defeated by Matilda's forces. But she was so unpopular that she was not crowned queen. Stephen was weak and lost land in France. One bright point was that lots of new churches and monasteries were built in his reign.

A modern historian writing about Stephen.

SOURCE E

Henry is honest, has good table manners and is generous. Our king is a peaceful man, but wins in war. He works very hard and is always trying to improve how the country is run.

Henry has taken a lot of land. No one is kinder to the sick and ill and no one is friendlier to the poor. The death of Becket was a mistake.

From a description of Henry II by Peter of Blois, written at the time.

SOURCE F

Henry II brought good times to England. England was well governed. Trade with other countries was good. There was only one revolt in 1173–4, and that was easily crushed.

A modern historian writing about Henry II.

Facts and opinions

When we look at sources, it is important to think about what are facts and what are opinions. If you think that something is a fact, you might be able to trust it more. If you think it is an opinion, you need to find out more about who the opinion belongs to!

TASKS...

1 In pairs, look again at Sources C to F.

   (a) Choose three facts (something that is true) from these sources and write them down.

   (b) Now choose three opinions (someone's view) from the sources and write them down.

EXTENSION TASK...

2 Use the information about Stephen and Henry to design book covers for these books:

   • The Reign of Stephen of Blois.

   • The Reign of Henry II.

Design one cover each. Remember to use useful pictures. Think about the message you want to put across. Was your king a good person? Was he a bad person?

When you have completed your cover, show it to your partner and explain your design. Then let your partner explain his or her design.

Plenary

If you were going to make a Hollywood blockbuster about Stephen of Bois and Henry II, which actors would you choose to play them? What big event from their lives would you use in your film? Why?

RICHARD I OR JOHN: WHICH KING WAS BETTER?

Objectives

By the end of this section you will be able to answer these questions.
- Have historians been too kind to Richard?
- Did John really deserve his bad reputation?
- Who was the better king: Richard or John?

By examining the sources, you will be able to:
- judge Richard I and King John
- compare the two monarchs and come to a final decision about who was the better king.

Starter

In this section we will be looking at two kings. One is remembered as being a good king. One is remembered as being a bad king.

Key word

Reputation How you are seen or judged by people in general.

*Think about someone famous. Do they have a good or a bad **reputation**? What has the person done to get their reputation?*

Feedback your results to the rest of the class. Now see if you can together answer the following question:

Does a person always deserve their reputation?

Richard I and John

SOURCE (A)

Richard I, who was King of England from 1189 to 1199.

When Henry II died in 1189, his son, Richard, became king. In films and TV programmes about Robin Hood, Richard is shown as being a good and brave king. His nickname was Richard the Lionheart. But, the truth about Richard is not quite so clear. He spent a lot of his time abroad fighting in the Crusades.

💡 Why do you think Richard I was known as Richard the Lionheart?

Richard's brother, John, who was king from 1199 to 1216, has a different image. He is usually shown to be a bad king.

King John, who was King of England ruled from 1199 to 1216.

TASKS...

1 (a) Look at Sources C to F, which are pictures about Richard I and John. Study them carefully. They will help you to decide who think you was the better king. The notes below will also help. **WS**

Stage 1: thinking about sources
When we think about sources, we need to consider:
- What type of source is it (for example, a painting, a drawing, a letter, a poem and so on)?
- Who produced the source and when?
- Why was this source produced?

Stage 2: how to study pictures
When we look at pictures we need to ask certain questions:
- What is the person who drew or painted the picture trying to show?
- Was the person who drew or painted the picture there at the time?
- Is the person who drew or painted the picture trying to make things up?

(b) With a partner, try to find answers to the questions above for each source.

Richard I and King John: the evidence in pictures

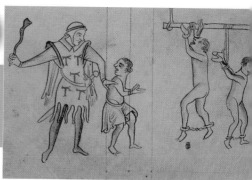

A picture of one of John's officials, drawn by a monk, who wrote about John in 1235.

SOURCE D

Richard I jousting with his enemy Saladin. The truth is that these two men never met.

SOURCE E

A picture from the thirteenth century called 'The flight of Richard the Lionheart from the armies of Philip Augustus'.

An artist's impression of John signing the Magna Carta.

TASKS...

1 (a) Look at Sources G to O, which are things that historians have written about Richard I and John. They will help you to decide who you think was the better king. **WS**

When we read written sources we need to ask certain questions.

- What is the historian who wrote the piece trying to say?
- Was the historian there at the time?
- Is the historian trying to make things up?

(b) On a page in your exercise book, write the heading: 'Richard and John – the main issues'. For each source note the key words to show the main issues of Richard's and John's reigns. An example has been done for you. **WS**

Richard and John: the main issues

Source G   Relations with the Church.

Source H

Source I

Richard I and King John: the written evidence

Richard didn't argue with the Head of the Church, the Pope. John's big mistake was that he argued with the Church and the barons at the same time. In 1208 the Pope shut down England's churches. In 1213 John had to apologise and give in to the Pope's demands.

A modern historian's opinion of King John and Richard the Lionheart.

When king, Richard I only visited England twice. Both times he came simply to raise more money for his fighting abroad. By the time Richard died, he had made England a poor country.

From a modern history textbook.

Richard did not have much to do with Wales, Scotland or Ireland. John married his daughter to a Welsh prince.

From a modern history textbook.

The French king, Philip II declared war on John. John's armies were defeated by the King of France in 1204 (and he lost Normandy). His hopes of getting back his land were destroyed.

A modern historian's account of John's reign.

SOURCE K

When Richard was away, the country was run well by the Archbishop of Canterbury. Knights were given more responsibility in day-to-day government.

A modern historian's comment on changes during the reign of Richard I.

SOURCE L

Richard died without an heir, but John had several children. However, John was not kind to children. He had his nephew, Prince Arthur, killed because he was worried that Arthur might try to claim the throne.

From a modern textbook.

SOURCE M

In 1192, Richard was returning from the Crusades when he was taken prisoner. He was kept for two years, until he bought his release using money raised in England.

From a modern textbook.

SOURCE N

When John became king, England was a poor country. So he made the barons he didn't like pay high taxes. War broke out between the barons who supported John and those who hated him. In the end, the barons that hated John forced him to sign the Magna Carta in 1215. The Magna Carta aimed to protect their rights.

- No taxes could be asked for without the permission of the barons.
- Nobody would be imprisoned without first having a fair trial.
- The barons would meet in a Great Council to advise the king.

John made it clear he was forced to sign the Magna Carta, and he persuaded the Pope that it should be ignored.

A modern account of the troubles faced by King John.

Richard was a great soldier and a great Crusader. He led the Third Crusade. He did what all great kings at the time had to do.

From a modern textbook.

TASKS ...

1 What was the Magna Carta?

2 How did the Magna Carta change the relationship between the king and the barons?

3 In groups, look at the key issues in your charts or in your exercise books. Now decide who dealt best with the main issues, Richard or John.

4 Was your choice for Task 3 also the better king? Explain your answer.

Plenary

Think of two new nicknames – one for Richard I and one for John. Discuss in your groups why you think they are good nicknames.

HENRY III OR EDWARD I: WHICH KING WAS BETTER?

Objectives

By the end of this section you will be able to answer this question.
• Who was the better king – Henry III or Edward I?

You will be able to:
• judge Henry III and Edward I
• compare the two monarchs and come to a final decision about who was the better king.

SOURCE A

Queen Elizabeth II, the current Queen of the United Kingdom.

SOURCE B

The British Parliament today.

Starter
Take a look at Sources A and B. Who do you think is more powerful today – the Queen or Parliament? Give reasons for your answer.

In this section you will find out about a big fight between the king and Parliament during the Middle Ages. The fight was over who had power.

Henry III

Henry III and Edward I both ruled for a long time. Henry was king from 1216 to 1272, and his son Edward ruled from 1272 to 1307. They had very different personalities. Henry was religious, and was more French than English. Edward was clever and energetic. His nickname was 'Longshanks' because of his long legs!

Henry III, who was King of England from 1216 to 1272.

TASKS...

1 Read about Henry III on page 155. Jot down what you think are the six most important events. Don't forget to make a note of the dates of these events.

2 (a) Write out a timeline for your six dates. Put the date first, then write a sentence explaining what happened. **WS**

(b) Now give each event a score. Your scores can go from +5 for a very good event to -5 for a disaster. Using crosses, plot your events onto a graph like the one opposite. When you have plotted your events, draw a line that links all the crosses. **WS**

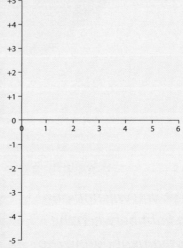

Plot the dates of your six events along this line, beginning with the earliest date first.

The life of Henry III

Henry III became king in 1216 at the age of nine. For the next eleven years, he was told what to do by his guardians. From 1227, he was old enough to rule without the help of others.

Henry was not very popular because he had many French friends. He had a very good relationship with the Church, but he gave the top jobs in the Church to foreigners. He also spent lots of money building churches.

One of Henry's problems was that he was not very successful at fighting wars. In 1229, he fought for Aquitaine in France, but lost.

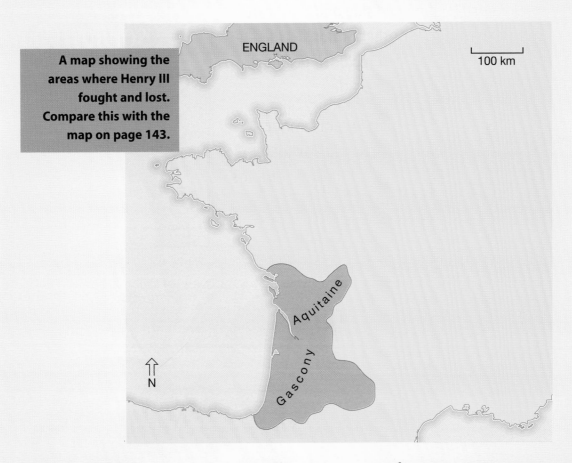

A map showing the areas where Henry III fought and lost. Compare this with the map on page 143.

Henry's wars cost too much money. This money came from increasing taxes, which didn't please the barons. They decided to demand change. Led by Simon de Montfort, Earl of Leicester, the barons met in Oxford in 1258. They agreed to limit Henry's power in a document called the Provisions of Oxford.

- A council would advise Henry. From now on he could not make decisions without the barons' agreement.
- Taxes would be decided locally, not by the king.
- Changes would be made to the royal household.
- The king, as well as his officials, had to promise to keep to these rules.

💡 How do you think Henry would have felt about these rules?

By 1261, Henry had had enough. He decided that he would ignore the Provisions of Oxford. In 1263, civil war broke out with Henry and his son Edward leading one side and Simon de Montfort leading the other. Simon decided to set up a Parliament that included ordinary people who did not have a title.

💡 What difference would it have made having ordinary people in a Parliament? Would they have wanted different things to the nobles and barons?

Simon de Montford was beaten at the Battle of Evesham in 1265, and in 1267 the civil war ended.

Simon de Montfort .

Edward I, who was king of England from 1272 to 1307, seated with bishops and monks.

Edward I

Edward I let Parliament make more descisions than his father. This was because he wanted money from it for wars in England and abroad.

Why did Edward go to war against the Welsh?

Some Welsh leaders said that Wales should be free from English rule. The leaders of this movement were Llewelyn, who was the Prince of Wales, and his brother David. In 1278, they started a war against the English. Edward fought back hard and in 1282 Llewelyn was killed in battle.

Why did Edward go to war against the Scots?

Edward I also went to war against the Scots. After the death of the Scottish queen, Margaret, in 1290, there was no clear successor to the throne. The Scottish nobles asked Edward to choose their king. In 1292 he chose John Balliol. Many Scots did not like Edward interfering in their affairs. So in 1295 they turned to France for help. Edward was very angry and sent an army which defeated a Scottish army at the Battle of Dunbar in 1296. A Scottish lord, William Wallace, continued the fight against Edward and defeated the English army at the Battle of Stirling Bridge in 1297. But by 1304 Scotland had been conquered and brought under the control of the English king.

Why did Edward go to war against the French?

In 1294, 1296 and 1297, Edward led unsuccessful expeditions to France to regain Gascony. But the French king gave it back anyway in 1303, because he had other matters to deal with.

Why did Edward argue with the Pope?

Edward also argued with the Pope. In 1296 the Church in England stopped giving Edward money because the Pope told it not to. Edward showed how unhappy he was about this by seizing church land. The Church backed down and he got his money.

Edward and Parliament

Edward improved how Parliament worked. In 1295 he called a Parliament that included all sorts of people. But Edward still had problems. The barons did not like having to pay high taxes.

TASKS...

1 Read about Edward I on pages 157–8. Jot down what you think are the six most important events. Don't forget to make a note of the dates of these events. **WS**

2 (a) As you did for Henry III, write out a timeline for your six dates. Put the date first, then write a sentence explaining what happened.

(b) Now give each event a score. Your scores can go from +5 for a very good event to -5 for a disaster. Using crosses, plot your events onto a graph like the one you did for Henry III (see page 154). When you have plotted your events, draw a line that links all the crosses.

3 According to your graphs for Henry III and Edward I, who was the most successful king?

Plenary

Imagine if the Queen ran the country today and there was no Parliament. How would life be different? **WS**

WHO WAS THE GREATEST KING OF THEM ALL?

Objectives

By the end of this section you will be able to answer this question.
- Who was the best king – William Rufus, Henry I, Stephen of Blois, Henry II, Richard I, John, Henry III or Edward I?

You will make a decision about who was the best king of all. You will also judge how good all the other kings were and decide which king was the worst of all!

TASKS...

1 Working in groups, you will decide who you think was the best king. **WS**

(a) Make a list of all the kings you have studied in this chapter. For each one, think about how well they did in these categories:

- Dealt well with neighbours.
- Had a male heir who could take over as king.
- Had peaceful relations with the Church.
- Good with the country's money.

- Good at running the country.
- Successful in war.
- Not many rebellions against him.
- Had a strong personality.
- Had few challenges to the throne.

(b) Now give each king a score for each category. You should award scores like this:

9 or 10 marks	Outstanding in this area.
7 or 8 marks	Has performed very well in this area.
5 or 6 marks	Has done a good job.
3 or 4 marks	Has not done so well, but is not a disaster.
1 or 2 marks	Is close to a disaster.
0 mark	A disaster!

If there is no information about a category, give a score of 5.

TASKS...

The 'lucky' mark

Some kings were luckier than others. Some became king at a good time, other kings took over a bad situation. So you can give the kings a 'luck' mark: –5 means you feel they have been unlucky, 0 means they have been lucky.

Add all the scores up for each king. The king with the highest score is the winner!

2 The class decides!

(a) Each group in the class should name their best king.

(b) Vote for your favourite king. You can vote for any of the kings. You do not have to vote for your group's decision.

(c) Collect the votes together and add them up. Now you will have an answer to the key question: *'Who was the best and who was the worst king, 1087–1307?'.* **WS**

3 Write a paragraph with the title *'Best king from 1087 to 1307'.* Draw a picture of the king, then write three points to explain why he is the best.

EXTENSION TASK...

4 Look again at the scores your own group produced for each king. Think about the king who scored the fewest points. Write a report on the worst king to explain why you think he is the worst king of them all. **WS**

WHAT WAS LIFE LIKE IN THE MIDDLE AGES?

In this chapter we will be looking at the quality of life in the medieval period. In many ways, this depended upon who you were and the position you held in society. The pace of life in the medieval period was much slower than the pace of life today.

💡 *Many people think that the pace of life at which we live today is very fast. What do you think they mean by this? What could we change to make life slower?*

For people in the medieval period, life was very different from life today. So the things that they considered important to a happy life were probably quite different. However, the ability to live a secure and happy life would have been just as important to them as it is to you today.

💡 *Based on what you already know about the Middle Ages, can you think what would have been important to a medieval person living a secure and happy life?*

Not everything about medieval life would have been different to life today. The decisions people had to make in order to earn a living in the Middle Ages were similar to the decisions people make today.

- "How do I earn a living?"
- "What can I buy?"
- "What can I sell?"
- "What skills do I need?"
- "Who else do I need to consider?"
- "What am I allowed to do?"

- "When can I say what I think?"
- "Where am I allowed to go?"
- "What can I do to improve my standard of living?"
- "What laws do I need to obey and why do I need to obey them?"

Before you start this chapter, choose some of the questions you have just read and write down some answers in rough. When you finish this chapter come back to the answers and see if, by understanding about people in the past, you can or need to alter some of your original answers.

WHAT WAS IT LIKE TO LIVE IN THE MIDDLE AGES?

By the end of this section you will be able to answer these questions.
- How did people in the Middle Ages live?
- Why did different people have different ways of living?
- Why did who you were matter more than what you were?

You will also investigate how people in the Middle Ages:
- viewed each other
- spent their days.

Starter

We live in very different times from the people who lived in the Middle Ages. There are lots of things in our lives that we feel are very important. We feel we could not do without them.

Make a list of ten things that you feel you could not be happy without. Compare your list with others in the class.

'Was everyday life in the Middle Ages hard?'

Day-to-day life

Not everyone today is a millionaire and lives in a big house. Some people find living from day to day difficult. People in the Middle Ages were very like us – some people had more than others. What was it like for different people? You will investigate this using some sources. You might want to look back at the diagram of the feudal system on page 59 to remind you of society's structure.

The king's life

His work

After William the Conqueror was crowned King of England in 1066, it was important to him that he could show he was in control. He began to build castles all over England to show that the Normans now ran the country. The Tower of London was the first of these castles.

The king's life was not always easy. Not everyone liked him, especially the Anglo-Saxons. Building castles was a way of showing that *he* now controlled the country.

The Tower of London, William the Conqueror's first castle.

His home

The king's life was very comfortable. A king would have lived in the best home. People at the time judged how important someone was by what they owned. For the king, it was important that he had the best home. So his palaces were richly decorated with tapestries. These added colour and kept out draughts.

Kings used to eat with up to 150 people in the great hall. But they became so rich they could afford to have their own rooms where only family and guests ate. A real luxury was a private toilet called a garderobe. Really, this was just a hole in a bench with the waste falling outside the castle walls!

SOURCE B

The Great Hall, Penshurst Palace, Kent.

His food

The king would only have eaten the best that was available.

SOURCE C

Food for a royal family of eight and all their servants at Kings Langley in 1290. This menu doesn't list any bread, vegetables, fruit, herbs and spices or pastry used in the meals.

A FEAST DAY
Half a cow
1 and a half calves
1 sheep
1 pig
Half a wild boar
2 kids
6 chickens
12 pigeons
450 eggs

A FISH DAY
200 salt cod
300 herrings
3 conger eels
5 smoked eels
576 ordinary eels
1 pickerel
13 and a half litres of oysters
Whelks
Trout
Salmon

TASKS...

1 Use the evidence to describe what life was like for a king during this time. Write down some key words.

SOURCE D

We held court, collected rents and kept buildings in good order. We also checked on the activities of the locals.

The work that a lord of the manor did.

The lord of the manor's life

His work

The king could not run the country alone. He needed lords he could trust to rule in his name. These lords were not as rich as the king. But, compared to ordinary people, they had a lot of money. Their job was to keep local people in order and raise taxes for the king.

WHAT WAS LIFE LIKE IN THE MIDDLE AGES?

His home

In the years after the Norman conquest, England became more peaceful. Lords did not have to defend themselves in strengthened castles. By the end of the thirteenth century, castles were being replaced by more comfortable manor houses.

These buildings were much smaller than castles, but they still had defences like a moat, gatehouse and tower. The rooms were smaller and the windows were bigger. Glass, which was very expensive, was used to block out the draughts. Having glass showed that you were very rich.

The family's rooms were separate from the servants. They were designed for comfort, not safety. Outside, the large courtyard was used to entertain people. It was also an area to prepare defences, if necessary.

SOURCE E

Stokesay Castle, built in the late-thirteenth century.

His food

The lord of a manor could not eat as richly as the king. But it was expected that the manor house could show its wealth by being able to lay on fine banquets for special occasions. The death of a lord was marked by a grand meal at which invited guests celebrated his life, as Source F shows.

The Paston servants worked for days killing beasts, brewing beer, and cooking geese and chickens. The guests also ate 1000 eggs, 20 gallons of milk, 41 pigs and 49 calves.

A meal eaten at the funeral of John Paston in 1466.

TASKS...

1 Look at the evidence. Write down some key words that describe how lords lived.

2 Compare the lord's list to the one you made for the king.

In Oxfordshire in 1086, the richest peasants worked twelve acres of land. In return, they had to work on the lord's land every other day, either tending or ploughing it.

What a peasant had to do for the lord of the manor, as well as his own work.

The peasant's life
His work

For a peasant in a village, life would be very different to that of the king or the lord. Peasants worked on the land all year round. The jobs they did included ploughing, sewing seeds and harvesting crops. There were different jobs for different times of the year.

Peasants did not own their own land. They rented it from the lord of the manor. Peasants also had to work on the lord's **demesne**.

Key words

Demesne The land that a lord kept for himself.

His home

Peasant's houses usually had only one room. The whole family would eat and sleep in this room. The earth floor would be covered in straw. The smoke from the fire went out through a small hole in the roof. Sometimes, the family's animals would also share the house for protection at night.

His food

The food that peasants would eat was usually very simple.

SOURCE H

An artist's impression of what a peasant's home in the Middle Ages would have looked like.

SOURCE I

1–1.5 kg of bread

1.5 litres of ale

Vegetable stew

0.08 kg bacon or a herring (not every day)

Details of an ordinary worker's daily food intake.

TASKS...

1 Look at the evidence of what it was like to be a peasant in the Middle Ages. Write down some key words that describe a peasant's life.

2 Compare these words with the ones you listed for:
   (a) the king
   (b) the lord of the manor.

SOURCE J

We had beef, four calves, two sheep, veal, five lambs, six pigs, seven rabbits, eggs, butter, milk and cream, pepper, vinegar, cloves, sugar, dates and honey.

The food given to celebrate a saint's day.

Feast days

Feast days were special days when the lord of the manor might give food to everyone in the village.

TASKS...

1 Look again at the evidence of what life was like for the king, a lord of the manor and a peasant. Now draw a mind map like the one below, to show what you think it was really like to live in the Middle Ages. **WS**

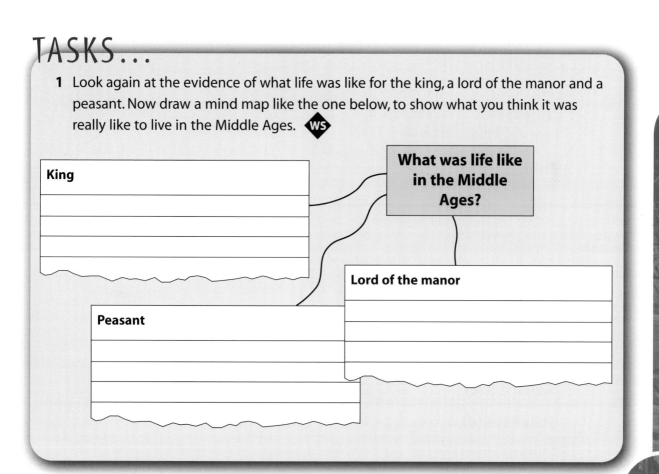

King

What was life like in the Middle Ages?

Lord of the manor

Peasant

The law

People had to obey strict laws in the Middle Ages. This helped the ruling class hold on to their power and influence.

TASKS...

1 Look at the statements below. Some of them contain facts (things that actually happened). Some of them contain opinions (people's views).

(a) 'Ploughmen, cowherds, shepherds and dairy workers should eat and drink only basic food.'

(b) 'Almost everything peasants needed had to be made at home or by one of the villagers. Every village had a blacksmith, a carpenter and other people who had special jobs.'

(c) 'I work hard all year so that I can give the lord the service he demands.'

(d) 'Tenants should pay rent. This should be either cash or crops.'

In pairs, decide if each statement is a fact or an opinion.

	Fact	Opinion
Statement **(a)**		
Statement **(b)**		
Statement **(c)**		
Statement **(d)**		

TASKS...

2 (a) In groups, discuss how you decided which statements are facts and which are opinions.

(b) Look again at the four statements. Who do you think would have thought these ideas?

Plenary

Look back at what you have discovered. In groups, choose either:

• the king
• the lord of the manor
• the peasant.

Write down five things you think would have made this person contented/happy.

How does this list compare with the list that you made at the start of the section? What are the main differences?

WHAT WAS LIFE LIKE IN THE COUNTRYSIDE?

Objectives

By the end of this section you will be able to answer these questions:
- Why did people want to challenge the king?
- What happened when people challenged the king?

You will also investigate:
- the problems peasants faced
- how different people felt about the decisions they had made.

Starter

Make a list of the rules in your school. Underline the ones that you think are the most important rules. Say why they are important.

Look at the rules you have underlined. Are there any occasions when you would break these rules?

What happened after the Black Death?

In 1348, England was hit by a plague called the Black Death. It killed almost half the people in the country. The peasants that survived soon found that their lords needed workers to look after the crops that were rotting in the fields. Many peasants saw a chance to demand higher wages for the work they did. Life began to get better for ordinary families.

For the lords, life since the Norman Conquest had been comfortable in many ways. They had land, wealth, power and influence. The Black Death was a great shock. There were no longer enough peasants to work on the land. The lords had to listen to peasant demands for wages, or face losing their crops. Some peasants even demanded the freedom to work for other people.

By 1351 the government had had enough. It said that peasants should know their position in the country. It introduced a law called the Statute of Labourers. This said that peasants should not be paid any more than they were paid before the Black Death.

The peasants hated the new law because it stopped them earning higher wages. Nearly 30 years later, fourteen year-old King Richard II was to face the anger of the peasants.

King Richard needed money to fight a war against France. To pay for his army he introduced a new tax. Everyone older than fourteen had to pay this tax. People called it a head tax, or 'poll' tax. Whether you were rich or poor, you had to pay exactly the same amount.

The peasants were angry. Thomas Brampton, a tax collector was lucky to escape alive when he tried to collect village taxes. Soon after, the peasants went from village to village asking people to join them in saying no to the tax.

Statute of Labourers

The king knows that peasants are refusing to work without high wages.

– It is demanded by the king –

- *all workers should work for normal wages*
- *workers not willing to work will be put in prison.*

The Statute of Labourers, introduced in 1351.

The peasants soon found leaders – Wat Tyler and John Ball. Ball was a priest who said that all men were equal to each other. Many peasants agreed with him.

John Ball talking to the peasants in 1381.

The peasants decided to revolt. Thousands of them marched on London. They wanted to challenge the king and his advisers. They burned some rich people's houses and murdered some advisers.

The king decided to meet the rebels and Wat Tyler at Smithfield. At the meeting, Tyler drew a dagger. The Mayor of London thought he was going to kill the king, so he killed Tyler. The king acted quickly. He told the peasants to go home. He said he would grant their demand to be set free.

The peasants went home, but the king changed his mind. He tracked down leaders of the rebellion, and had them hung. The heads of Tyler and Ball were hung on spikes on London Bridge as a warning to others who wanted to rebel against the king.

The king was angry with the peasants. He said, 'You are still peasants. You will stay as slaves, but now life will be harder for you.'

TASKS...

1 Why do you think peasants wanted to challenge the king? List your reasons.

2 Now share your reasons with a partner. Add to your list any new reasons that you come up with together.

3 King Richard told the peasants that they would 'stay as slaves'.
Draw a chart in your book like the one below.

The lords	The peasants

Write down as many words you can think of to describe how the two groups would have felt about King Richard's words. Try to avoid using the word 'angry' on either side of your chart.

4 Do you think the king made the right decision? Explain your answer.

EXTENSION TASK...

5 At the end of the Peasants' Revolt, King Richard said:
'You are still peasants. You will stay as slaves, but now life will be harder for you.'
Imagine you are King Richard. Write your own version of the Peasants' Revolt. Make sure that you:

- give a clear opinion
- use the information you have found to support your opinion
- reflect on what you have said by writing a final comment.

Plenary

Look back over this section.

- Which rules do you think the king really wanted to keep?
- Who do you think should make rules?
- Who do you think rules are for?

WHAT WAS LIFE LIKE IN A MEDIEVAL TOWN?

Objectives

By the end of this section you will be able to answer these questions.
- Why did people choose to live in a medieval town?
- What types of jobs did people do?
- What problems did people have?

You will investigate:
- why towns were popular
- what skills people needed to live in a town
- how difficult it was to earn money in a medieval town.

Starter

Why do you think most people choose to live in a town instead of a village? In pairs, write down four reasons why people might choose to live in a town today.

Compare your ideas with others in your class until you have a list of eight reasons. Try to put your reasons into groups.

The growth of towns

In the Middle Ages, most people lived in villages. As England became more peaceful, the population of the country grew. People wanted to live in a better way and they wanted more goods. They had to come together to trade for the goods they wanted, so towns began to grow for this reason.

What charters did

Medieval kings also liked towns. No one could hold a market without the king agreeing to it. In return for taxes, he gave towns charters. These charters gave towns the right to hold a fair or a market. The bigger the town grew, the more money the king received.

A town receiving a charter, which allowed it to hold markets and sometimes fairs.

Town	£s paid to the king
Boston	1100
Bristol	2200
King's Lynn	770
Lincoln	1000
London	11000
Shrewsbury	800
York	1620

Tax paid to Edward III by towns in England in 1334.

TASKS...

1 **(a)** On a map of Britain, find the towns named in Source B.

(b) What do you think these figures tell us about towns in the Middle Ages?

Towns soon became richer than the villages and began to attract more people. A charter allowed a town to charge strangers visiting it. Laws were made to stop townsfolk being cheated when they bought things. Traders were punished if they were caught cheating!

SOURCE C

A punishment for a trader who has cheated his customers.

Differences between towns and villages

In villages, people worked hard in the fields. In towns it was easier. People opened stalls that made them money. They spent this money on things like clothes and shoes. So new trades began to cater for these new demands. Streets in towns were often named after the trades found, like Shoemaker's Row.

People's names began to change as well. With so many people, it became common to say what the person did, as well as their name. So, for example, Thomas the baker, became Thomas Baker.

TASKS...

1 **(a)** Using the example of Thomas Baker, what sort of jobs did these people do in the Middle Ages? You may need to use a dictionary to find some of the meanings of the last names.

- Richard Fisher
- Peter Smith
- Mary Thatcher
- William Mason
- Matilda Taylor

(b) List any other last names you can think of that might have come from the jobs people did.

The importance of craft guilds

If things were made badly, people would stop buying them. The craftsmen of the towns wanted to make sure that only the best goods were sold. So they formed groups called guilds to do this.

Each guild had its rules. You could not be a member of the guild unless you followed the rules and became an **apprentice**.

Rules of the workshop

1 The master is the boss.

2 To become a master, you must work for seven years as an apprentice.

3 At the end of seven years you must pass a test.

4 The test will be to make a masterpiece.

5 If you pass you can become a master and employ apprentices.

6 If you fail, you can still work for yourself, but you will not be a master craftsman.

7 To protect yourself from problems of illness and old age, you pay a small sum of money to the guild every year.

Key words

Apprentice Someone who is learning a trade.

If any member becomes poor (through old age or sickness) or loses things in fire, flood or theft, the member shall have one and a half pennies per week from the guild fund.

What one guild did to help its members.

On the feast of Corpus Christi, all members shall come together to the guild feast.

Rules of St Michael Guild, Lincoln.

Guilds also organised entertainment for the town. They did plays based on Bible stories. Source E shows that going to these feasts was part of a guild's rules.

SOURCE F

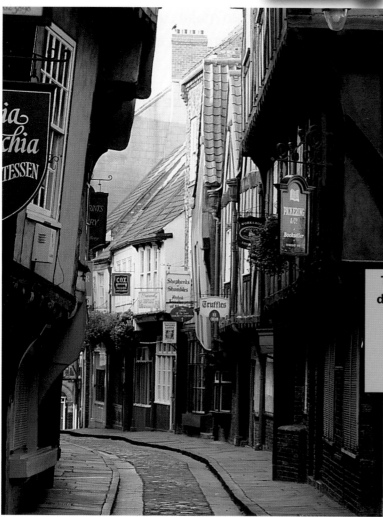

The Shambles in modern-day York. The shops would have been different in medieval times, but the layout would be practically the same.

The town fair

The highlight of the year would be the town fair. This would attract merchants from a wide area (including other countries).

Traders wanted their stalls in the busiest places so they could sell lots of goods. People began to set up shops on the high street. These shops had rooms behind to make the goods. These high streets still exist today.

TASKS...

1 Read pages 176–180 again to remind yourself about life in a medieval town. Remember your list of the reasons why people might choose to live in towns today? Now list the differences between town life today and town life in the Middle Ages.

2 Draw a mind map like the one below to show what life was like in a medieval town. **WS**

Draw lines between the boxes to link things that are connected. On the connecting lines, write a reason why you have connected them. Explain your connections to a neighbour. Then let your neighbour explain the connections that he or she has made.

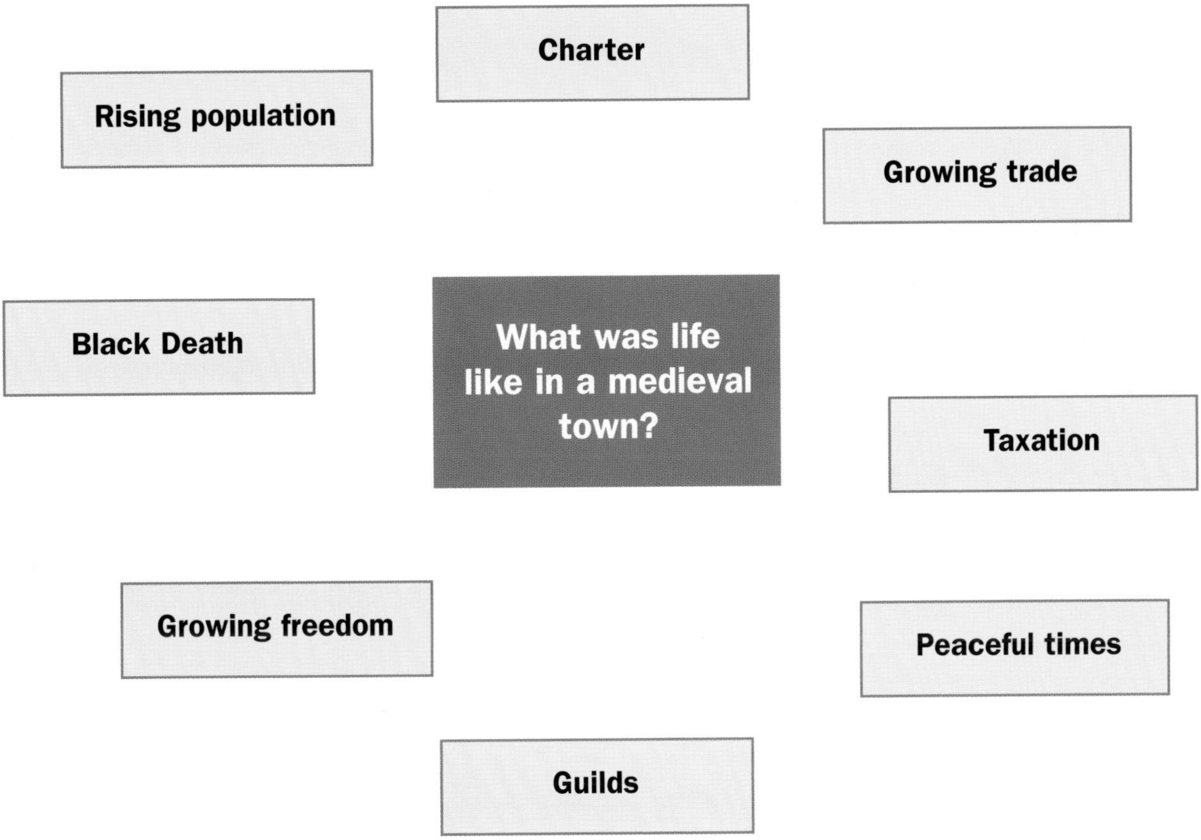

Charter

Rising population

Growing trade

Black Death

What was life like in a medieval town?

Taxation

Growing freedom

Peaceful times

Guilds

Plenary

Look back at what you have found out about people living in a town at the beginning of this chapter. How many of those reasons were the same for people that lived in a medieval town? Are there any differences? Why do you think this is?

HOW DID THE SYSTEM OF LAW AND ORDER CHANGE?

Objectives

By the end of this section you will be able to answer these questions.
- How did the law change in the Middle Ages?
- Why did punishments change?

You will also investigate:
- the types of crimes people committed
- how people were brought to trial
- the types of punishment in the Middle Ages.

Starter

Every society needs to have laws. But societies change, so laws need to change too.

You have been asked to decide on the guilt of a person. He is charged with the theft of another person's clothes from a sports centre.

Draw a three-point spider diagram and place the following questions on each point.

💡 *What do I need to know?*

💡 *How can I find out if someone is guilty?*

💡 *What punishment would I give to someone if they were found guilty?*

Now fill in answers to these question. Compare your answers to others your class.

Law in the Middle Ages

In the Middle Ages, the law was very different to the law today. There were different types of courts for different people. Priests were tried in Church courts. The most common court was that run by the lord of the manor's official, so it was called a Manorial Court.

SOURCE A

- John Joce let a stranger stay in his house.
- Agnes, who was poor, had a baby when she wasn't married.
- Nicholas didn't plough his lord's land very well.
- Robert's dog ate a young horse.
- Hugh dug holes in the road near his house.

From a local court record.

The Manorial Court was a simple court. Twelve men of the village were chosen to be the jury. They had to decide the outcome of arguments. Source A gives some examples of what they would be asked to judge. Members of the jury were not popular. They gave out hard punishments.

💡 What do you think the word 'crime' means?

💡 Look at the first three crimes in Source A. Why do you think they are not crimes today?

💡 Look at Source B. Who are these crimes against?

Criminals, crimes and punishments

Crimes were very different to today. Owing money, especially to the lord of the manor, was serious. People could be brought before the court for many things. They could be punished in many ways.

SOURCE B

Crime	Punishment
Selling rotten meat.	Put in the pillory.
Lying under oath.	One year in prison, but to be put in the stocks every three months.
Using false dice to trick people.	Put in the pillory.
Placing an iron in a loaf of bread.	Put in the pillory.

Examples of medieval crimes and the punishment that was given.

SOURCE C

A pillory and a stock, used as a punishment for some medieval crimes.

TASKS...

1 What do you think these punishments were supposed to do to someone who was caught?

2 Why do you think people who committed these crimes were treated like this?

It was not easy to catch people committing a crime. Criminals had to be caught in the act! Local people had to deal with criminals, because there were no police. If a villager was the victim of a crime, he would 'raise a hue and cry'. Then the rest of the village would try to catch the suspect.

People were made to be responsible for each other's behaviour. The village was divided into groups of ten, called tithings. If one of them committed a crime, then the others had to make sure they went to court, or they all would be fined.

In some cases, finding someone guilty was easy. Source D gives an example of a **capital offence**. In other cases guilt had to be proved by God. One method was trial by ordeal. Look at Source E.

Key words

Capital offence A crime considered worthy of death or severe punishment.

SOURCE D

Wakelin killed Matilda Day with a knife. The people of the village, and twelve jurymen, say that he was caught in the act with a bloodstained knife. He is to be hanged.

From the trial of Wakelin, the son of Ranulf.

SOURCE E

Heat the water until it is boiling. If only one person says he is guilty, the accused should put his hand in the water up to the wrist. If there are three, then it should be up to the elbow. Then wrap up the hand, and after three days undo the bandages to see whether the wound has begun to heal.

Trial by boiling water AD 930. People thought you were guilty if your wound did not heal.

Another way of proving guilt or innocence was trial by combat or battle. Look at Source F.

💡 Why do you think it was difficult to catch medieval criminals?

💡 What do you think a 'trial by ordeal' was?

Trial by battle, from the Hampshire Court Records, 1249.

Justice

Look at the story below and on page 186. It happened in Hampshire in 1240. It's a long story. Try to remember as much as you can. **WS**

In 1249, a man of Winchester had some clothes stolen. People of the town raised a hue and cry, and several groups of local men were rounded up.

A jury of twelve local men heard the evidence from those who were accused of the crime. Everyone knew that if anyone was found guilty, they would be hanged. This was because the clothes were worth over a shilling in value.

The men accused of the crime were brought before the court and the evidence was presented to the jury. It was difficult to make out who was telling the truth. Each group of men seemed to have been somewhere else at the time the clothes were stolen. It was going to be difficult to prove someone guilty, because some men would not say anything. Anyway, the jury did not really want to hang someone for such a small sum of money.

'This happens all the time,' said one of the locals. 'Everyone needs clothes. If you leave them lying around, the you know what will happen.'

Over the next few days, the sheriff asked lots of questions. Eventually one man said he had stolen the clothes. Walter Bloweberme was known to be a rogue in the area, and with people asking too many questions he decided to own up.

Shaking, Walter stood before the sheriff. 'Yes I did it, but I wasn't alone and I'm not going to be hanged without a fight!'

'So who was with you?' The Sheriff asked. 'Hamo Stare,' said Walter. 'We both did it. We broke into the house and took all sorts of things. But it was Hamo who took the clothes. He said they would suit him.'

The sheriff waited. 'How do I know you are telling the truth? For all I know, Hamo could be innocent.' Walter stared at the sheriff. 'If I'm lying, then let God decide. I'll take Hamo on and you'll see if I am telling the truth.'

This was trial by battle. The law said that if one man accused another, they could fight until death or until one confessed. The sheriff looked at Walter, 'So be it. Trial by battle. May God have mercy on your soul if you are lying.'

It was not long before Hamo Stare was arrested. He denied stealing the clothes and agreed to the trial. The men were given leather suits, shields and a weapon. The sky was clear on the day of the battle and a small crowd gathered to see the men take their places on the battle field. It would not take long. Both men knew that they were fighting for their lives. Whoever lost would either die in the fight or be hanged later in the day. God would decide.

The two men attacked each other, blows smashing down on the shields that the men held. In minutes it was over. Hamo, exhausted by the fight, collapsed in a heap, weeping.

Justice had been done. Walter had been telling the truth and God had seen that he had won the day. For Hamo, a few hours of life were left before he was hanged.

TASKS...

1 Develop a storyboard to show the story you have just read.
Use pencil to sketch out the frames. **WS**

EXTENSION TASK...

2 Use your storyboard to write out the story as clearly as you can using your own
words. Finish the story by saying if you agree or disagree that fighting is a good way
to decide if someone is guilty. Explain your decision. **WS**

The king's interest

The law slowly began to change. The
king began to order that a jury should
judge people. This was not just because
he wanted to be fair. Look at Source G.

SOURCE **G**

Money was one of the main reasons why
people were tried. The king kept the
fines paid for minor offences, and
anything owned by that person who
was to be hanged.

From a modern history book.

TASKS...

1 **(a)** What reasons do you think the king had for passing laws in the Middle Ages?
Write down as many reasons as you can.
  (b) Now write down as many reasons as you can why we pass laws today.
  (c) Compare your two lists.

Plenary

Why do you think that laws change over time?

Make a short list of all the things we have today that makes
proving a person's guilt easier than in medieval times.

If we did not have these things, what changes would we need to
make to our laws? Does this explain the ways in which people
were proved guilty of a crime in the Middle Ages?

WHY DID MEDIEVAL PEOPLE TRAVEL?

Objectives

By the end of this section you will be able to answer these questions.
- Why did medieval people travel?
- What were the problems of travelling?
- Why did travel become popular?

Starter

How many times have you heard someone in your family say: 'The car's broken down again'? In the Middle Ages this wasn't a problem. Engines hadn't been invented!

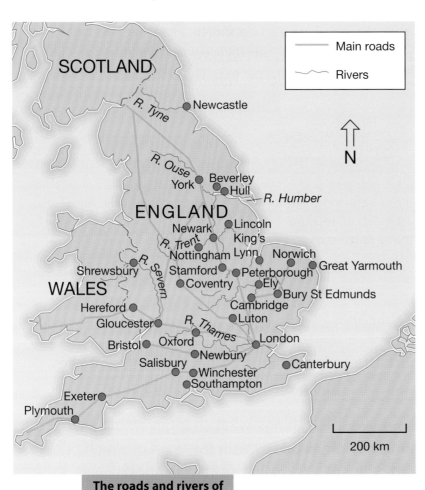

The roads and rivers of medieval Britain.

What changes do you think would happen to your town if there were no cars or lorries? Write a list of how it would affect you for one week. Now write a list of how it would affect you for one year. What are the differences between the two lists?

CHANGING TIMES 1066–1500

Travel in the Middle Ages

Most people in the Middle Ages did not need to travel further than ten miles. There was just no need to. As long as they could get to the local market, they could buy most of what they needed. For anything special, there were travellers who visited the villages. There was no need to risk the dangers of the open road.

Medieval roads were nothing like the ones we have today. There were fewer of them and many were in poor condition. Most were just dirt tracks. These were impossible to travel along in wet weather or snow, because they turned into mud.

Travelling on roads was also risky. Roads into towns were not lit, and people travelled very slowly. Because of this, they were easy targets for thieves. It became so dangerous to travel by road that in 1285, the king ordered that all the bushes and trees on each side of a road had to be cut down. This was to stop thieves hiding.

SOURCE A

Even if someone was willing to risk the journey, there was the problem of knowing exactly where you were. Few people could read or write, so there was little point in having signposts to guide a traveller's way. Anyone wanting to travel was either familiar with the route or asked locals as they passed through a village. Travellers even had their own saint to protect them, St Christopher.

The problems of travelling in 1450.

SOURCE B

160 persons and more, with long swords and other weapons, hid under a large hedge next to the highway and lay in wait for William Tresham from midnight to the hour of six, at which time William appeared. They attacked him and he died. And they gave him many more deadly wounds and cut his throat.

This explains the problems of a traveller from Northampton to London in 1450.

Not everyone travelled by road. Many goods were brought to England by ship. From the ports, some goods were loaded onto boats that sailed along the major rivers of the country. When the river became too shallow, or a different route was needed, all the goods had to be unloaded. Then road transport was the only option.

SOURCE C

Most people who travelled were wealthy or made a living from travelling, like traders. They carried goods on packhorses. They visited different towns, providing all the goods that the people of a local area could not get for themselves.

Packhorses carrying wool.

Travellers often lose their way, so knots are made in the branches of trees and bushes to mark the highway.

A traveller's description of road markings in 1400.

Goods were sold in markets or at fairs held once or twice a year. So many traders and travellers went to fairs that they became special events. People came from all over the area to buy the finest silks, cloth and rare spices. They swapped stories and listened to news over a jug of ale at the many inns in the town.

SOURCE E

A rich merchant.

SOURCE F

Inns were not places to stay in for long. They were dirty and flea-ridden. But travellers could meet up with others there, and so have company for the dangerous journey to the next town.

Travellers arriving at an inn. They had to share bedrooms with strangers.

Even the royal family found travelling difficult. Kings liked to be seen by the public, and made journeys around the country. Along with the king were all his servants and bodyguards, making the trip difficult to plan.

A painting of a royal carriage in the Middle Ages.

SOURCE G

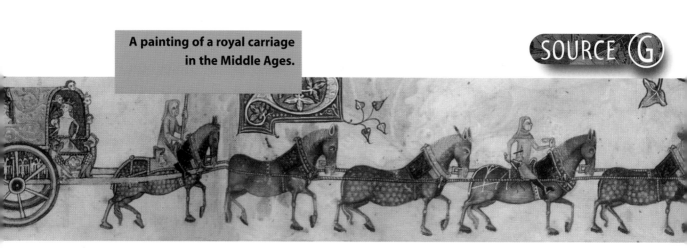

SOURCE H

The king would travel in a well-guarded but bumpy carriage along the best-used tracks of the country. The nobles would ride on horseback. The group would cover up to 40 kilometres a day. This was faster and safer than walking, but slower than a single horseman.

Travelling by foot in the Middle Ages.

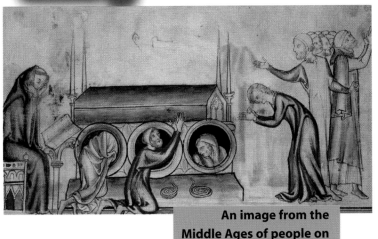

An image from the Middle Ages of people on a pilgrimage.

Some people travelled for religious reasons. The Church encouraged travellers to seek out holy objects (like saints' bones) in places such as Canterbury Cathedral. Along the way, monasteries were expected to open their doors to weary travellers. They provided a basic meal and a bed. This was not much, but at least it was shelter from the dangers of the open road.

TASKS...

1 Using the information from this section, create a medieval snakes and ladders travel game.

   (a) Draw out a 30 cm by 30 cm box. Divide it into 100 squares by drawing lines across and down every 3 cm. Number all the squares in a zig-zag up the board. Remember that to play the game, the numbers must follow each other. **WS**

21	22	23	24	25	26	27	28	29	30
20	19	18	17	16	15	14	13	12	11
1	2	3	4	5	6	7	8	9	10

   (b) In square 1, write the name of your town. In square 100, write the name of a town far away. This is where your travellers will be going.

   (c) On your board you now need to have five snakes (five problems) and five ladders (five good things). Look at what you have found out from this section. Write down on a piece of paper your 'snakes' and your 'ladders'.

   (d) Decide which was the worst problem and make that the longest 'snake'. The problem that will cause your travellers the least problems will be your shortest 'snake'. Do the same with your 'ladders'. The event that will help your travellers most will be the longest ladder.

   (e) Have a go at playing your game!

EXTENSION TASK…

2 Using the snakes and ladders game that you have made, write a diary of your travellers' experiences. WS

Plenary

The number of people living in England during the Middle Ages was very low. It was fewer than 5 million people. Today our population is over 58 million. Draw a Venn diagram like the one below, showing the advantages and disadvantages of travelling in *modern* Britain. In the overlap put any factors that are both good and bad.

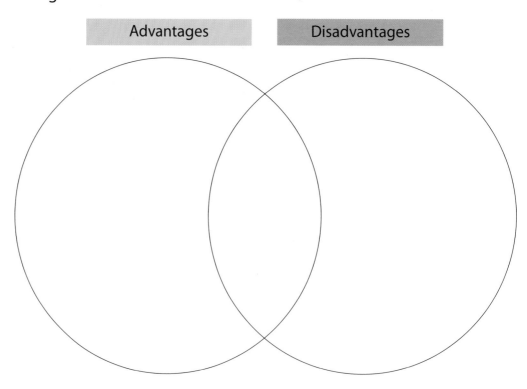

| Advantages | Disadvantages |

How would this diagram be different for the Middle Ages? Draw another Venn diagram and now put in all the advantages and disadvantages of travelling in *medieval* Britain.

WHAT COMPARISONS CAN WE MAKE ABOUT LIFE IN THE MIDDLE AGES AND LIFE TODAY?

Objectives

By the end of this section you will be able to answer these questions.
• How was everyday life in the Middle Ages different from today?
• Why was daily life hard for many people in the Middle Ages?
• Why was it difficult to change the way ordinary people lived?

Starter

How hard is your life?

Think about a normal week during term time. Work out carefully how many hours in a working week you spend in a classroom with a teacher. Don't count the breaks! How much free time during a week do you have?

What things do you need to think about to decide if life is hard or not?

Interpretations

🔦 Is this statement right or wrong?

🔦 How do you know?

'Everyday life in the Middle Ages was hard.'

In order to answer the question, you need to look at some evidence from the time.

SOURCE A

I work hard. I get up early and drive the oxen to pull the plough. Even when the snow is deep I must plough a full acre or my lord will be angry with me. I have a boy who helps me with the animals. He shouts and hits the animals to move when they stop. And I do more. I have to fill the oxen's bins with hay and water, and muck them out. It is very hard work, for I am not free.

A peasant's working day.

SOURCE B

A medieval painting of country workers.

SOURCE C

Plague victims being buried, 1349.

SOURCE D

The king needed more money to pay for the war in France. In 1377, he introduced a poll tax. Everybody over the age of fourteen had to pay.

Demands on a peasant.

💡 Look at Sources A to D. How do you think they help us to understand life for ordinary people living in the countryside?

Remember that more people lived in the countryside than lived in towns.

💡 Look at Sources E and F, then compare them to Sources A to D. What things are the same?

I have been round all the material shops in Norwich and I can't buy any cloth good enough for a dress. Everything is too simple in colour and quality. Would you please get me three metres of something you think would suit me? Choose whatever colour you like.

A letter from a rich woman to her husband.

There was no dressing up, no music, no singing. There were no loud sports. Only board games, chess and card games were allowed.

A description of how the death of the master of the house affected the Christmas celebrations.

💡 When you use sources, what do you need to think about?

Think about the following.

- What type of source is it (a letter, a painting, a poem)?
- Who produced it and when?
- Why was it produced and who for?

Historians have problems knowing what the lives of ordinary people were like. This is because most people could not read or write. There was nothing that we would use today to record sound, so what we know of the everyday life of these people we have to get from sources that show them going about their normal lives.

TASKS...

1 (a) Read the following poem. It comes from the fourteenth century.

*I have no penny to buy **pullets**,*
nor geese nor pigs, but [I have] two green cheeses,
*a few **curds** of cream, a cake of oatmeal,*
two loaves of beans and bran, baked for my children;
but I have parsley and pot herbs and plenty of
cabbages,a cow and a calf.

This is the little we must live on till the
***Lammas** season.*
*Poor folks in **hovels**,*
charged with children and overcharged by landlords,
what they may save by spinning they spend on rent,
on milk, or on a meal to make porridge.

> ## Key words
>
> **Pullets** Young chickens.
>
> **Curds** Solids from milk.
>
> **Lammas** The period of time from 1 August to 29 September.
>
> **Hovel** A small miserable house.

(b) With a partner, think about the 'message' the poem tries to put across. In your book, write down any questions about the poem.

2 Draw a mind map like the one below. Use the rest of the information you have read in this chapter to say whether you think things did or did not change over this period. Give at least one reason for your decision. **WS**

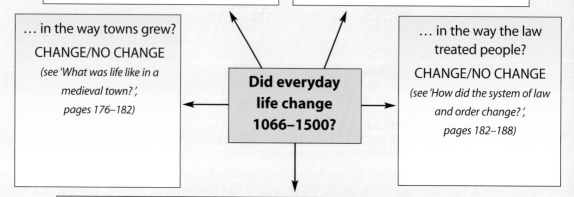

… in the way that people lived?
CHANGE/NO CHANGE
(see 'What was life like in the countryside?', pages 162–171)

… in the way that people were treated?
CHANGE/NO CHANGE
(see 'What was life like in the countryside? ', pages 172–176)

… in the way towns grew?
CHANGE/NO CHANGE
(see 'What was life like in a medieval town?', pages 176–182)

… in the way the law treated people?
CHANGE/NO CHANGE
(see 'How did the system of law and order change?', pages 182–188)

Did everyday life change 1066–1500?

… the way travel affected people?
CHANGE/NO CHANGE
(see 'Why did medieval people travel?', pages 188–194)

TASKS...

3 You have been invited to spend a week in the Middle Ages. You need to think carefully about your reply. Draw a Venn diagram like the one below to show:

- your reasons for wanting to live in the Middle Ages in one circle

- your reasons for not wanting to live in the Middle Ages in the other circle

- aspects you are not sure about in the overlap area.

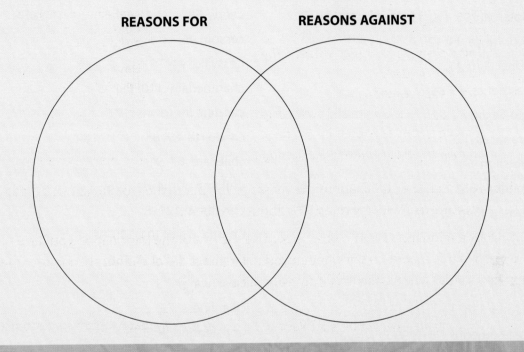

REASONS FOR   REASONS AGAINST

EXTENSION TASK...

4 Do you agree or disagree with this statement:
'Everyday life in the Middle Ages was hard.'

Plenary

Given all the evidence on pages 161–197, do you think you would like to have lived in this period of time? List the reasons for your answer.

Index

A

abbess 106
abbots 64, 106, 110, 111
Alfred, Prince 11, 12
almoner 110, 112
anaesthetics 85, 86
Anglo-Saxons 7, 22
apprentices 179
archbishop 64
astronomy 83
Athelstan, King 5, 8, 11

B

bailey 69
Ball, John 174
barber-surgeons 78–9, 99
barons 59
Bayeux Tapestry 44
beliefs 101–32
Bible 121, 179
bishops 64
Black Death 75, 76, 172–3
blood letting 79

C

Canterbury, Archbishop of 64, 117, 151
Canterbury Cathedral 114, 118
Canute, King 8, 11–12
castles 68–71, 166
cathedrals 65, 101
cavalry 19

cellarer 110, 112
Celts 6
ceorls 58
cesspit 96
Cessville 94–7
chamberlain 110, 111
charters for towns 177
childbirth 87, 88
childcare 87–91
Children's Crusade 126
Christians 121–8
Church 63–6, 101, 130–1
civil wars 142, 151, 156
clean water 75
cleanliness 75
Constantinople 126
convents 13, 106
coroners 90–1
cottars 58
countryside life 172–4
courts 182–3
craft guilds 179
crime 183–4
Crusades 75, 120–8

D

Danes 11
demesne 167
diseases 82
dissection 75, 85
doctors 81–6, 99

Domesday Survey 60

Dunbar, Battle of 157

E

Earls 58, 60

Edgar the Atheling, Prince 18, 20, 28

Edgar, Prince 55

Edward, King (the Confessor) 8, 11–14, 20, 22, 25–6

Edward I, King 154, 157–8

Edward the Atheling 14, 20

Edwin, Earl of Mercia 36, 51

Eleanor of Aquitaine, Queen 142

Ely 51, 65

Emma, Queen 11, 19

English army 22, 31, 35

Evesham, Battle of 156

Exeter 52, 55

F

fairs 180, 191

family trees 13, 134

feast days 169

feudal system 47, 57–61

four humours 82, 84

friars 64, 116

Fulford Gate, Battle of 36, 42

fyrd 31, 35, 39, 41

G

garderobe 164

germs 82

Godwin, Earl 12, 13

Godwin, Edith 12–13, 22

Godwin, Gyrth 40, 43

Godwin, Gytha 52

Godwin, Harold *see* Harold, King

Godwin, Tostig 21, 37

Great Council 151

Great Hall 164

guilds 179

H

Hadrian's Wall 7

Harald Hardrada 20–1, 28, 29, 32, 35–8

Harefoot, King 8

Harefoot, Prince 11–12

Harold, King (Harold Godwin) 14, 22, 25–6, 28, 30, 42–9

Harrying of the North 55

Harthacanute, King 8, 11–12

Hastings, Battle of 39–41, 43–5, 48–9

head tax 173

Henry I, King 137–40

Henry II, King 117–8, 142–4

Henry III, King (Longshanks) 154–6

herbal mixtures 84

Hereward the Wake 50–2, 55

hospitals 77–8

housecarls 29, 31

hue and cry 184

hygiene 93–7

I

infant deaths 88, 89, 90–1

infirmarian 110

inns 191

invasions 6, 35

Islam 121

J

Jerusalem 114, 121–8
Jews 102, 121
John, King (Lackland) 146–50
Judaism 121
jury system 183, 187

K

kings 13, 18–22, 133–65
kitchener 110, 112
knights 59, 61, 116
Koran 121

L

landholders 60, 61
law 182–7
lepers 77
lord of the manor 165–7, 169

M

Magna Carta 133, 149, 151
Magnus, King of Norway 20
manorial court 182–3
manors 60
Matilda, Princess 140, 141–2
medicine 75–86, 98–9
mercenaries 31
midwives 88
miller 116
miracles 130
monasteries 106, 108–12
monks 64, 106–8, 116
Morcar, Earl of Northumberland 36, 51
motte 69
Muslims 121–2, 123, 125, 126–8

N

Norman army 19, 31
Norwegian army 32
novices 110
nuns 64, 106–8, 116

O

oath of loyalty 19, 25, 26

P

packhorses 190
palisade 69
Parliament 156, 158
peasants 60
Peasants' Revolt 173–5
Penshurst Palace 164
Peter of Blois 138, 139–40, 144
Pevensey 40
pilgrimages 113–6, 193
plague see Black Death
poll tax 173
Popes 25, 64, 117, 118, 122–3, 158
precentor 110, 111
priests 63, 64
printing 75
prior 110
privy 97
Provisions of Oxford 155–6
punishment 183–7

R

rakers 96, 97
relics 131
religious beliefs 102–5
Richard I, King (the Lionheart) 122, 146–8,
    150–2

Richard II, King 173–5
rituals 131
roads 139, 189, 190
Roman Catholic Church 102
Roman Empire 5, 7
royal travel 192

S

saints 130
St Christopher 130
St Thomas Becket 114, 116, 117–9, 142–3
St Thomas's Day 118
Saladin 125, 126, 148
Scandinavia 8
Scots 157
Senlac Hill 43, 49
serfs 58
sewage 96, 97
Simon de Montfort 155–6
sinews 85
sins and punishment 102, 104
squire 116
Stamford Bridge, Battle of 37–8, 42
Statute of Labourers 173
Stephen I, King (Stephen of Blois) 141–2,
        144
stockade 69
Stokesay Castle 166
Stone Age 6
subregulus 14, 22
supernatural beliefs 129–31
superstition 82, 130
surgeons 86

T

thegns 58, 60

thieves 189
tithings 184
Tower of London 163
towns 93–7, 176–80
traders 190, 191
travel 188–93
trial by combat 185, 186
trial by ordeal 184, 185
Tyler, Wat 174

U

urine tests 83

V

Varangian Guard 20
Vikings 5, 8, 21, 32, 38
village life 178
villeins 59, 60

W

wall paintings 103, 104
war 28–32, 35, 150, 155, 157
water seller 96
Welsh 22, 157
Wife of Bath 116
William II, King (Rufus) 137–9
William the Conqueror, King (William of
        Normandy) 18, 19, 25–6, 28–31, 35, 40,
        47–74
wimple 106
Winchester Cathedral 65, 66
Witan 14, 22
woad 6

Y

York 36, 37, 55, 180